Software Reliability

Macmillan Computer Science Series

Consulting Editor: Professor F. H. Sumner, University of Manchester

G. M. Birtwistle, *Discrete Event Modelling on Simula*

Richard Bornat, *Understanding and Writing Compilers*

J. K. Buckle, *The ICL 2900 Series*

Derek Coleman, *A Structured Programming Approach to Data**

Andrew J. T. Colin, *Programming and Problem-solving in Algol 68**

S. M. Deen, *Fundamentals of Data Base Systems**

David Hopkin and Barbara Moss, *Automata**

H. Kopetz, *Software Reliability*

A. Learner and A. J. Powell, *An Introduction to Algol 68 through Problems**

A. M. Lister, *Fundamentals of Operating Systems, second edition**

Brian Meek, *Fortran, PL/I and the Algols*

Derrick Morris and Roland N. Ibbett, *The MU5 Computer System*

I. R. Wilson and A. M. Addyman, *A Practical Introduction to Pascal*

* The titles marked with an asterisk were prepared during the Consulting Editorship of Professor J. S. Rohl, University of Western Australia.

Software Reliability

H. Kopetz

Technical University of Berlin

First published 1979 in the United Kingdom by
THE MACMILLAN PRESS LTD
London and Basingstoke
Associated companies in Delhi Dublin
Hong Kong Johannesburg Lagos Melbourne
New York Singapore and Tokyo

Typeset in 10/12 Press Roman by
Styleset Limited · Salisbury · Wiltshire
and printed in Great Britain by
Unwin Brothers Limited
The Gresham Press
Old Woking, Surrey

British Library Cataloguing in Publication Data

Kopetz, H
    Software reliability. — (Macmillan computer
    science series).
    1. Computer programs — Reliability
    I. Title
    001.6'425   QA76.6

    ISBN 0–333–23372–7
    ISBN 0–333–23373–5 Pbk

Contents

Preface

This book is intended for the student of computing and the practising computer professional who is concerned about the unreliability of computer systems. It is the author's aim to bring an understanding of the concept of software reliability and to impart some ideas, which should lead to the development of more reliable software systems. The book tries to bridge the gap between theory and practice and will thus be valuable supplemental reading for a course on software engineering.

During my work on real-time systems in industry I have seen many occasions where the subjects of testing, error detection and error handling have been tackled in an unsystematic, *ad hoc* fashion which leads to subsequent problems in the integration phase. The chapters on these subjects formed the starting point of this book and other chapters were developed in order to produce a clear and concise text covering the whole subject of software reliability, while always keeping the practical aspect in mind.

This English edition is a revised version of the original German edition. The author would like to thank all his friends and colleagues for their help, suggestions and remarks on the German text. Many of the comments which have been raised have been considered in this revised English version.

Particular thanks go to Mr Williams, for the assistance in the translation of the manuscript, and to the editor of Carl Hanser Verlag, Mr Spencker, and the editor of Macmillan, Mr Stewart, for their kind co-operation. Above all, I would like to thank my wife Renate for her constant encouragement and help.

Berlin,
January 1979   H. KOPETZ

1 *Introduction*

'As long as there were no machines, Programming was no problem at all; when we
had a few weak computers, Programming became a mild problem, and now we have
gigantic computers, Programming has become an equally gigantic problem.'

E. W. Dijkstra (1972b) p. 861

With the first generation of computers the problems in programming were blamed
on the severe constraints imposed by the hardware of that time. Since then there
have been tremendous technological advances in the field of computer hardware.
But although the hardware has become much more flexible, the problems with
programming have not decreased; on the contrary, they are worse now than they
ever were before. The physical constraints of the hardware have been replaced
by the invisible constraints of the capacity of the human mind. The neglect of
these psychological limits, together with a disquieting optimism, has led to the
design of large software systems. It is not until these very complex logical systems
are realised that the incompleteness and inconsistencies of the human intellect
show up and result in a number of errors. Each one of these errors can be considered as a single logical flaw without any relation to the whole. Experience
shows, however, that all these errors, if seen as a whole, describe a general
phenomenon commonly referred to as the 'software crisis'. The complexity of
many software systems has become unmanageable, and the natural consequences
are delays and unreliability.

There are considerable economic implications connected with the unreliability of software. Between one-third and one-half of the effort that goes into
the development and maintenance of a software system is spent on testing and
debugging. Since during the implementation of a large computer system, more
resources are allocated to the software than to the hardware, the direct costs
of the software unreliability themselves amount to a substantial fraction of all
computer costs. If, in addition, the indirect costs of errors (for example, lost
benefits of a system) are considered, then the economic significance of software
reliability becomes even more pronounced.

There are a number of methods by which more reliable software systems
can be produced.

(1) By a design methodology which leads to a highly reliable product. If we
    were successful in finding such a design methodology we could completely
    eliminate — in theory at least — all activities which are connected with

testing, debugging and run-time error treatment. This alternative, the constructive approach to software reliability, precedes all other methods and must be considered the most effective approach to software reliability. In the past few years, a considerable amount of effort has been spent in the development of improved software design techniques. Although some promising results have been achieved it is to be doubted that a design methodology in itself is sufficient for the development of software systems of the required reliability.

(2)   By testing and debugging. This method assumes that the required reliability of a software product can be achieved by very thorough testing and debugging. At the present time more effort is spent in the testing and debugging phase than in any other phase of the software development process. In spite of this, the problem of the unreliability of software has not been solved satisfactorily. This can be attributed to the fact that, even during a very thorough test, only a small fraction of all possible input cases of a software system can be executed.

(3)   By the inclusion of redundancy in order to detect and correct errors which show up during the use of a software system. This last method is distinctly different from the previous methods. It is assumed that a complex computer system will always contain errors and steps are taken to reduce the consequences of such errors.

This book is based on the assumption that reliable software can be developed most effectively by a combination of all three methods. The main emphasis is put on software for on-line, real-time systems, since in these systems the consequences of errors and failures are normally much more serious than in systems for batch processing.

2 Basic Concepts

2.1 RELIABILITY

Every technical system is developed with the intention of fulfilling a particular function. A measure of how well this function is performed is given by the capability of the system, which does not normally give any indication of the period for which the system runs without cause for complaint. The capability as a function of time, depends on reliability and maintainability.

The systematic investigation of reliability starts with the realisation that the reliability of a system may be defined as a probability.

The reliability of a technical system is the probability that the system performs its assigned function under specified environmental conditions for a given period of time.

It is synonymous with the probability of survival of a system. Quantitatively it may be described by a reliability function, $R(t)$, which gives the probability that a system will function over the time interval $(0, t)$. It has the following properties.

$R(0) = 1$; the system is certain to function at the beginning
            of the interval.
$R(\infty) = 0$; at time $t = \infty$ the system is certain to have failed.

In the interval $(0, \infty)$ the function decreases monotonically.

The unreliability $Q(t)$ of a system is defined as the probability of failure, hence

$$Q(t) + R(t) = 1$$

Next the concept of effectiveness is introduced. A system is said to be effective when it not only performs its allotted task, but also operates over a long period. The effectiveness as a function of time is not only dependent on the reliability, but also on the maintainability (figure 2.1).

The maintainability of a system is the probability that, after the appearance of an error, the system is returned to an operational condition in a given time. The average time taken to correct an error is known as the 'Mean Time to Repair', abbreviated to MTTR. This interval starts at the appearance of the error and

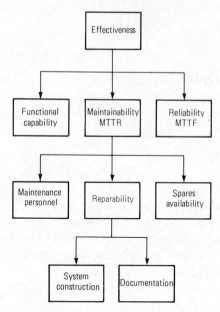

Figure 2.1 Interrelationship of functional capability, maintainability and relia-bility

ends when the system becomes operational again. Maintainability depends on a number of factors; the availability and competence of maintenance personnel, the availability of spare parts, and the ease with which the system may be repaired, that is, reparability.

The reparability of a system is the probability that an error will be repaired in a given time, by service personnel of average ability, assuming that spare parts are available. While maintainability is also a function of the service organisation, reparability is a system characteristic, that is, it depends on system construction, documentation, and so on.

Of interest in practical applications is the Mean Time Between Failures (MTBF). Strictly speaking, such a mean only has any relevance if the failure rate over a long period (in comparison to the MTBF) does not change. In such a case the conditional probability of failure during any given interval is constant. (The condition is that the system is functional at the beginning of that interval).

The MTBF is made up of two terms, the Mean Time To Failure (MTTF) and the Mean Time To Repair (MTTR) that is

MTBF = MTTF + MTTR

Since the MTTR is generally small in comparison to the MTTF, MTBF is often in practice taken to be synonymous with the MTTF.

System availability is defined as the percentage of the time, during a given interval, that the system is in fact available, thus

$$A = \frac{\text{MTTF}}{\text{MTTF} + \text{MTTR}}$$

A high availability can be achieved by a very small MTTR compared with a relatively short MTTF, as well as a longer MTTR for a larger MTTF (figure 2.2). The availability alone is thus not sufficient to characterise completely the relationship between effectiveness and time; in many cases the actual number of failures may be the decisive factor.

Redundancy

If a system contains more resources than are absolutely necessary for the fulfilment of its task, it is said to contain redundancy. The term 'resources' is here taken in its broadest sense, and in a computer system can mean hardware, software or time (Avizienis, 1972).

As a measure of redundancy the following relationship is introduced (Neumann *et al.*, 1973, p. 15).

$$r = \frac{\text{additional resources}}{\text{minimum necessary} + \text{additional resources}}$$

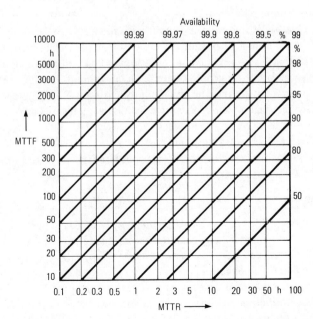

Figure 2.2 Relationship between maintainability (MTTR), reliability (MTTF) and availability

Redundancy is necessary for the detection and correction of faults. During the design stage of a system it is possible to choose between two completely different alternatives in order to increase the reliability of a system. High reliability may be achieved either without redundancy by using high quality components, or by using a greater number of average quality components redundantly.

Active redundancy is employed when the redundant components take an active part in the normal system operation. Standby redundancy is employed when the redundant system parts are only switched on when the active parts of the system drop out due to a failure.

If it has been decided to increase system reliability by means of redundancy, then a choice has to be made between redundancy at component or at system level. For the same amount of additional resources, redundancy at the system level offers a smaller increase in reliability than at the component level. The use of redundancy at component level, however, places greater demands on the engineer. Protection against error propagation in systems with redundancy at component level requires a greater development effort than in systems with redundancy at system level.

2.2 PROGRAMS AND PROCESSES

The terminology used thus far has been developed for, and applies primarily to, the reliability of equipment, that is, hardware. Implicit in this is the assumption that a system that functions correctly initially will eventually fail due to the ageing of its components.

The situation is somewhat different with software. There will be no failures due to ageing, failure will be due to design errors. A design error in part of a program will first lead to observable symptoms when that part of the program is actually executed with appropriate input data. Thus, the relationship between the static program text and the dynamic execution of the program is of great importance when dealing with software reliability. The following model has been substantially influenced by Denning (1971), Dijkstra (1972a), Goos (1973), Horning *et al.* (1973), and King (1971).

A program may be thought of as an ordered set of instructions or statements

$$\langle S_1, S_2, S_3, \ldots, S_m \rangle$$

The instruction space of the program is made up of elements of this set.

The execution of a single statement is called an action or elementary process. An action can be considered under two aspects, the transformational aspect and the control aspect.

The transformational aspect deals with the transformation of information stored in the computer memory. Each action can be considered as a function operating on a number of variables

$$x_1, x_2, \ldots, x_n$$

which assume input values from the domains

$$D_1, D_2, \ldots, D_n$$

and results from the ranges

$$R_1, R_2, \ldots, R_n$$

The Cartesian product

$$D = \underset{i=1,n}{X} \; D_i$$

is defined as the input space

$$R = \underset{i=1,n}{X} \; R_i$$

as the output space and the union of the input space and output space as the data space of the action. The variables are called input variables and output variables of the action respectively.

The control aspect of an action deals with the definition of the successor statement. There are two types of binary relations between statements. Statement 2 is the immediate successor of statement 1 and statement 2 takes as input the result of statement 1. The integer variable, which designates the successor statement is called the program counter j where

$$1 \leqslant j \leqslant m$$

In our model we distinguish between three kinds of executable statements.

(1)   The execution of an assignment statement (assignment action)

$$x_k, f(x_1, x_2, \ldots, x_n), j$$

causes the value of the variable x_k to be changed according to the result of the function f. The successor statement to be executed is the immediate successor in the instruction space.

(2)   The execution of a test and branch statement (test and branch action)

$$P(x_1, x_2, \ldots x_n), j_1, j_2$$

involves the examination of a predicate P over the input variable which is either true or false. If it is true, the successor statement is j_1, otherwise j_2.

(3)   The execution of a halt statement (halt action) terminates the execution of the program.

At certain well defined instants of time the state of the sytem can be described by a state vector

$$v = \langle a_1, a_2, \ldots, a_n, N \rangle$$

where $a_1, a_2, \ldots, a_n, N$ define the values of the program variables $X_1, X_2, \ldots,$ X_n, and the program counter respectively. The set of all possible states of the state vector is the state space of the system.

We call a program a program module if it contains one and only one halt statement, if the last element of the ordered set of statements is this halt statement and if the instruction space is not modified during the execution of the program. It is assumed that the execution of a program module is started at the first statement of the instruction space. In the following the terms program and program module will be used synonymously.

The relationship between a program and its execution can be described on four different levels of abstraction.

(1)   Given an initial state vector v_0 we consider the sequence of state vectors

$$v_0, v_1, v_2, \ldots, v_r$$

generated during the execution of the module. This sequence of state vectors is called a computation generated by this module. The control path of a computation is defined as the sequence of values of the program counter.

(2)   If we abstract from the specific data transformation aspect and consider only the sequence of actions

$$a_1, a_2, a_3, \ldots, a_r$$

performed during the execution of the module, provided there is an initial state vector v_0, we get an action sequence of that module. A decision-free program module can generate only one action sequence but many different computations.

(3)   If we abstract from the specific data transformations and from the specific action sequences generated during the execution of the module and consider only the general data transformations under the assumption that the execution will start at the first statement and will terminate, we get the process which is generated by the execution of the program module. Each process is embedded in an environment which furnishes the inputs and uses the results. Any variable that is an input variable to any one action of the process is a significant variable of the process. Any variable that is an out-

put variable to any one action of the process is a changed variable of the process. An input variable of the process is every variable that is a significant variable of the process and a changed variable of the environment. An output variable of the process is every variable that is a changed variable of the process and a significant variable of the environment. All variables that are used in any one action of the process and that are neither input nor output variables of the process are internal variables of the process.

(4) If we abstract from the internal variables of the process and consider only the input variables, the output variables and the data transformation of the process, then the process can be considered as an elementary process or action on a higher level.

We thus have a recursive feature in our definitions. The execution of a program module can be considered as a computation, a sequence of actions, a process or an action on a higher level. The primitive element in our system is a basic data transformation. The above definitions are not necessarily restricted to the software levels. They can also be used to describe hardware processes. There are many common elements between hardware and software processes and in some respects a distinction is not justified.

Due to the recursive nature of the above definitions, the error analysis of a software system with a hierarchical structure may be reduced to the investigation of the behaviour of a single process.

2.3   CORRECTNESS, RELIABILITY AND ROBUSTNESS

It is assumed that no changes will be made to the software system, the correctness and reliability of which is being analysed. Clearly, every change to a software system creates a new system which will have different reliability properties from the original system.

Software Correctness

Software correctness is concerned with the consistency of a program and its specification. A program is correct, if it meets its specification; otherwise it is incorrect. When considering correctness it is not asked whether the specification corresponds to the intentions of the user.

Software Reliability

Software reliability, on the other hand, may only be determined when the actual utilisation of the software by the user is taken into consideration

'Reliability is (at least) a binary relation in the product space of software and users, possibly a ternary one in the space of software and users and time.' (Turski, 1974, p. 15.)

In the preceding section the relationship between a program and the process associated with it was discussed. A process may also be thought of as the realisation of a function that relates every point in the input space to a point in its associated output space. If there is an error in the process this realisation will not be achieved as intended, that is, various points in the input space will not produce the expected results. If a procedure is available (a so-called 'test oracle'), whereby it may be determined for every point of the input space whether the computation starting at this point delivers a result that corresponds with the intentions of the user or not, then we can introduce a binary error function $e(i)$ which is defined over the entire input space so that

$e(i) = 0$ the computation, that starts at point i, is correct
$e(i) = 1$ the computation that starts at point i is either incorrect, or does not terminate where $i = 1, \ldots, N$
and N = the number of points in the input space (MacWilliams, 1973)

For every application there is defined, over the complete input range, the distribution of input values such that

$\Sigma p(i) = 1$
$p(i)$ the probability that point i occurs in the input domain for the particular application

The probability of the appearance of a software error is then given by

$\lambda_n = \Sigma e(i)p(i)$
λ_n = probability of the appearance of a software error for an input case (Kopetz, 1974).

The choice of a particular input case, from the set of all possible input cases, is the desired random event. Software reliability may thus be defined as follows.

The reliability of software is the probability that a software system fulfils its assigned task in a given environment for a predefined number of input cases, assuming that the hardware and input are free of error.

In software systems, the selection of the input completely determines the output of a computation. Herein lies the fundamental difference from hardware reliability. With an error caused by ageing, it is not necessary to look at a particular input, since it can be assumed that the hardware originally functioned for all inputs, and the error lies in the breakdown of a hardware component (Avizienis, 1972). (The problem of design errors in the hardware logically belongs to the class of software errors.) The failure rate of software can only change when either the error function changes, that is, changes to the software are carried out, or the input distribution changes, that is, the program is placed in a new environment. An example of the varying error rates due to a changing input distribution is encountered in the commissioning of a software system. As soon as the test conditions change, the error rate changes by leaps and bounds (Wolverton and Schick, 1972).

If it is assumed that the input distribution does not change, and that the program is not modified, then the software error rate cannot change. Under these conditions software errors may be described by a constant error rate.

The relationship between the reliability defined as a function of time, and the probability of error for each of the input cases may be written in terms of the system input rate

$$\lambda_t = \lambda_n r$$

where λ_n = probability of the appearance of a software error for an isolated input case

      λ_t = error rate as a function of time

      r = number of input cases per unit time (input rate).

The same reasoning can also be applied to real-time systems. The time axis can be subdivided into discrete intervals that are defined by the cycle time of the computer. Timing starts from a defined initial condition of the system. Clearly the input range must be expanded with the time dimension. This additional dimension increases the complexity of a system significantly, as is known from common experience.

In a number of publications (Jelinski and Moranda, 1972; Shooman, 1976; Hamilton and Musa, 1978) reliability growth models for software have been presented. These models not only consider the reliability of a software system *per se* but look also at the change (hopefully growth) of reliability as a consequence of program modifications (error elimination). In the development of these models many assumptions about failure mechanisms, number of residual errors, program modifications and the use of the system have to be made. It has yet to be shown whether all of these assumptions are fully justified (for a criticism of some of these assumptions see Littlewood, 1978).

Software Robustness

The concept of software robustness is used to investigate the relationship between software and system reliability.

System reliability may be defined as the probability that the computer system performs its allotted task during a given period of time, under specified environmental conditions.

The term environmental conditions is taken to mean not only the physical environment surrounding the computer, but also the input distribution (and its rate) and the average number of input errors.

The definition of system reliability differs from that of software reliability in that it does not need the hypothetical assumptions of error-free hardware and correct input. The ability of the software to handle these different error types is known as software robustness, which may be defined as follows.

A software system is said to be robust when the consequences of an input or hardware error related to a given application are inversely proportional to the probability of the appearance of that error in that application.

To explain the concept of software robustness in more detail let us assume that an error is expected to occur with the probability p and will result in a cost C to the user. (This cost C is a measure of the error effect.)

A software system is robust if for all possible error types in a given application

$$C \sim \frac{1}{p}$$

This means that errors which are expected to occur frequently should only have a minor effect on the given application. In order to assess the robustness of a software system in a given application a list of critical error effects and of probable error causes must be available.

Robustness is a necessary software characteristic if a high system reliability is to be obtained. In the real world environment, input errors, hardware failures and errors in the software and possibly in the hardware are a fact of life and it is primarily during the design of the software that mechanisms can be developed in order to detect these errors and to reduce their impact on the given application.

3 *Errors*

An exact analysis and classification of the error types that can appear in a system is of central importance to the development of reliable systems. After such an analysis and classification it is possible to introduce measures which either reduce the likelihood of certain classes of error, or minimise the effects of such errors should they appear.

3.1 THE NOTION OF AN ERROR

Our language contains a number of different terms for indicating a deviation between the intended and actual state or behaviour of a system, for example, error, fault, failure, mistake, malfunction, deficiency, flaw, and so on. With each one of these concepts some specific attributes are commonly associated which make it difficult to use such a concept in a general context.

In order to avoid such semantic problems, the listed terms are used throughout this book with the following meanings.

error: deviation between intended and observed state or behaviour of a system. (This is the most general term)
failure: error during the operation of a system
fault: error in the hardware
mistake: human error

If we need to distinguish between the effect of an error and the cause of an error we shall talk about error symptoms and error cause.

An error can only be recognised to exist when conditions deviate from a predefined norm. The term error is thus a relative one which loses its meaning in the absence of either an explicit or implied norm. When differing norms are applied during the assessment of given conditions it is possible for these conditions to be classified as correct or erroneous depending upon which norm is used.

With software systems a reference norm may be drawn up from the system specifications, that is the functional requirements and the acceptance criteria. If no clear and unambiguous system specification exists, then during the acceptance of a software system implicit assumptions about the fulfilment of the system functions take the place of an objective norm. The subjective interpretation of these implicit assumptions has already in many cases led to serious misunderstandings.

3.2   CLASSIFICATION OF ERRORS

In the following section an attempt is made to classify, from various points of view, the errors that can appear in a computer system — especially the software — so that the basis for a unified treatment of different error classes can be established.

Software and Hardware Errors

The most common classification is the subdivision into software and hardware errors. Software errors consist of all errors that result from systems analysis or programming, and hardware errors result from the malfunction of the machine. Although at first sight this distinction is quite clear and unambiguous, there are borderline cases that are increasingly difficult to classify, since the boundary between software and hardware is becoming more indistinct; for example, an error in a microprogram of a Read Only Memory in the CPU, which in some cases causes the erroneous execution of a hardware instruction.

Classification According to Error Symptoms

The classification according to the immediate error symptoms is particularly significant, since this classification of an error may be directly performed, instead of having to use a difficult and complicated error diagnosis beforehand. When taken in conjunction with the input domain of a software system, the classification according to error symptoms may be made as shown in figure 3.1. The actual consequences of a particular type of error are heavily dependent on the requirements of the particular application. In general, type I errors (where the system recognises that it is unable to process the input) are not as serious as the other errors in figure 3.1. An exception to this is found in real-time systems, which must react to an input within a certain predefined time. In such a system the rejection of an input can produce catastrophic results.

Errors of types II–V are considered to be serious. Wrong results, in as much as they lie outside a tolerance band defined for the application, undermine the confidence of the user and make the system unusable. Perhaps not so critical, but equally serious, is the occurrence of a system breakdown. Since no more output is given by the system after a breakdown, it is necessary to plan for an error detection mechanism which is outside the given system.

Classification According to Error Cause

Every error in a computer system may be traced back to one of the following: erroneous system design in either the software or hardware, degradation of the hardware due to the environment or ageing, or erroneous input data (either operator mistake or actual data). Design, degradation and data errors form three orthogonal axes of an error space.

INPUT / SYSTEM REACTION	Outside the intended input domain (Input error)	Inside the intended input domain
INPUT REJECTED (System error detection)	CORRECT	TYPE I ERROR
WRONG RESULTS (Error detection outside system)	TYPE II ERROR (serious)	TYPE III ERROR (serious)
SYSTEM BREAK-DOWN	TYPE IV ERROR (serious)	TYPE V ERROR (serious)

Figure 3.1   Classification of errors according to error detection and the input related to the input domain

The classification into these three subdivisions is based on the cause of the error and not its effect. The classification therefore presupposes a complete and successful error diagnosis.

A design error occurs when, despite the correct operation of all components (with reference to their specification), and despite correct input data, the results of a computation do not yield what is intended.

A degradation error occurs when a system component, due to ageing or environmental influences, does not meet the relevant specification. Both design and ageing errors can occur in the hardware, but only design errors can occur in the software.

An input error arises from the incorrect operation of the system, that is, instructions in the relevant operating manuals are not followed, or the actual input data is wrong. It is one of the tasks of system design to define the reaction of the system in the event of erroneous input data. Figure 3.2 summarises the characteristics of these three types of error.

	HARDWARE ERRORS (Degradation)	SOFTWARE ERRORS (Design)	INPUT ERRORS
Error – cause	Ageing failure of components Environmental	Complexity of design Input distribution	Human mistake
Error rate as a function of time	Initial decrease – then constant (increase at end of life cycle)	Constant, assuming program and input distribution are also constant	Initial decrease (learning curve) then constant
Can this type of error be completely eliminated? theoretically/ practically	no/no	yes/no	no/no

Figure 3.2   Occurence of various types of error

According to this classification an erroneous element in a data base is either a software error or will lead to an input error. If the view is taken that the data base is part of the software system, then it is a software error. If however the data base is considered external to the software system, then this wrong data element will, if accessed, lead to an input error.

Classification According to Duration

A further classification of hardware and input errors may be made according to the duration of the error. An error that occurs from a particular time onwards and remains uninterrupted and repeatably in the system is a permanent error. If, however, only a temporary change in the system characteristics can be observed, after which the system seems to be completely normal again, this error is said to be transient. Even though of short duration, a transient error can have serious consequences for the further execution of a program. Since transient errors cannot be reproduced systematically, their diagnosis and removal can be difficult.

Transient errors in the hardware are often not distinguishable from software errors in their effects. For example, a fault that causes the negation of a bit, which can cause either the storing of erroneous data, or the execution of a wrong instruction, gives rise to a symptom that cannot be distinguished from a software error.

Internal and External Errors

Often, the immediate consequences of an error cannot be observed. Only when the effects of such an 'internal' error have propagated to a point where the output is influenced, can the error be observed from outside the system (Neumann *et al.*, 1973, p. 10). The distinction between internal and external errors is made in accordance with observability. If a system contains redundancy, not every internal error will necessarily lead to an external error. The consequences of a failure in a redundant system can be guarded against. The division into internal and external errors is heavily dependent on the error detection interface chosen in each particular case. For example, if the error detection interface has a hierarchical structure, the same error may be considered both as an internal or as an external error depending upon which level of the hierarchy is used as a reference. The distinction between internal and external errors is essential for the further analysis of reliability. In order to establish a defined position for the elimination of errors, measures are required which cause either the detection of all internal errors at specified error detection interfaces or the prevention of consequent external errors by the introduction of redundant system components. If an error is not detected within the system, that is, the error detection mechanism is outside the system, then this internal error may cause a serious system error, that is, wrong results, or a system breakdown (according to figure 3.1).

Classification According to the Consequences for the Application

The specification for complex systems, besides containing the primary functions which justify the implementation of the system from an economic point of view, often contain secondary functions that contribute to the effectiveness of the complete system. Should such secondary functions fail, the result will not be catastrophic for the user. However, an error is said to be critical when it results in the interrruption of the system primary function. If an error affects only the system secondary functions it is said to be non-critical. The division into critical and non-critical errors is only possible when a clear distinction has been made between primary and secondary functions in the system specification. For the development of reliable systems this distinction is of great significance, and more attention must, clearly, be given to critical errors. In certain cases it is possible, if not essential, to interrupt deliberately a secondary function in order to rectify a critical error that has occured. Fragola and Spahn (1973) have suggested an even stronger distinction than just between critical and non-critical errors. So that the consequences of an error may be classified, each error is given a number which indicates its severity.

Classification According to Development Stage

The development and use of a software system proceeds by a number of steps, each of which leads to a further development stage. The errors that occur can be classified according to the development stage in which they have been made (figure 3.3). A given result is thus only error free when a concrete solution can be assigned to a concrete problem; in other words, when every step in the development chain is correct. It is thus necessary to give each development stage approximately the same attention. Over-attention to one detailed area in the development, with the attendant neglect of other areas, will have a negative impact on the overall system reliability.

3.3   DESCRIPTION OF SOME SPECIAL ERROR AND FAILURE TYPES

Errors in Systems Analysis

In the real world problems do not appear in the form of mathematical equations. It is often necessary to adopt a protracted and iterative procedure to formulate a relatively abstract statement of a problem from the actual problem. In the technical as well as the commercial field this can often be the most difficult part of the development chain previously outlined. Each element that is of relevance to the problem has to be extracted from an abundance of information. As well as an in-depth technical knowledge, a systematic approach and a high degree of abstractive ability are required to achieve this challenging task. Errors that occur during systems analysis often only appear after the completion of the entire system, since there is no formal reference norm for this phase. Boehm *et al.*, (1975) report, from an error analysis which resulted from the commissioning of a complex software system, that substantially more errors were due to system analysis than to programming errors. A similar experience is quoted by Endres (1975); following an analysis of the DOS/VS operating system, half of all the errors encountered were due to misunderstanding the problem, and not due to programming. Programming errors are usually more easily recognised than system analysis errors.

In comparison to the formulation of an abstract statement of the problem, the development of an algorithm for its solution and the definition of an exact program specification are usually easier.

Programming Errors

A programming error is present when the object program deviates from the program specification. All errors, whether in the detailed implementation of logic, coding, or in the translation of this code, fall under this heading.

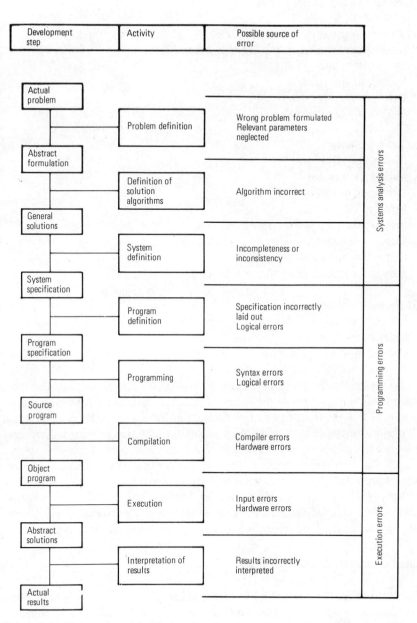

Development step	Activity	Possible source of error

Figure 3.3 The various steps in the development process and examples of possible sources of error (cf. Elspas et al., 1971)

Examples of Programming Errors

(1) During Design of the Detailed Logic
 Incorrect interpretation of the program specification
 Incomplete logic
 Neglect of special cases
 Deficient error handling
 Neglect of time consideration

(2) During Coding
 Syntax errors
 Initialisation errors
 Confusion of parameters
 Errors in loop counters
 Incorrect handling of results of a decision
 Multiple or non-definition of variables
 Errors in writing variable names
 Incorrect declaration of type and dimensions

(3) During Translation
 Compiler errors
 External symbols wrongly resolved
 Confusion of names of library programs

Concerning the frequency of programming errors there are very divergent statements, which are partly related to the unequal qualifications of programmers, as well as the varying degree of complexity encountered during programming. Clearly the programming methodology as well as the language chosen will strongly influence the number of program errors that occur.

Some data about the causes of software errors, detected within a three-year period after the commissioning of a real-time system, has been compiled by Boehm (1974a, p. 44) (figure 3.4). It is interesting to note that the number of logical errors which were detected in each of the three subsystems were inversely proportional to the time originally spent on systems analysis and design.

Data Preparation Errors

In practice, the error susceptibility of almost every data preparation method is a considerable problem. Human mistakes must be expected with the manual preparation of data on punched cards or other data preparation systems. Gilb (1973, p. 64) analysed the detailed error statistics for a typical commercial application (book-keeping), and found

approximately 3–5 per cent of all input records contain errors
30–40 per cent of all errors appear in a data field which carries cash items, and

Error source	Hardware diagnostic programs (%)	System software (%)	User software (%)
Unexpected side-effects after an alteration	5	25	10
Logical errors in design			
original	5	10	2
after alteration	5	15	8
Conflict between design and implementation	5	30	10
Sub total:			
logical errors	20	80	30
Writing errors	40	20	50
Hardware	40	–	20
Total	100	100	100
Total number of errors (detected within 3 year period)	36	108	18
Number of instructions	4k	10k	10k
Percentage of total effort for analysis and design	59	37	54

Figure 3.4 Classification of errors according to cause (Boehm, 1974a, p. 44)

are thus difficult to check
only a fraction of account number errors were detected through check codes.

The direct acquisition of data from analogue or digital sources can also result in errors, the probability of which should not be discounted. With tele-processing systems the data transmission can be a further source of errors (Martin, 1972, p. 285).

Execution Errors

The following cross section of the types of error that can occur during the execution should be considered in the light of the assumption that a correct object program with correct input data must lead to a correct end result. During the running of a program there are many opportunities for operator mistakes. The use of the wrong magnetic tapes or discs, incorrect initialisation of the operating system, or the wrong reaction to difficulties encountered with the system are typical examples.

In addition to these human errors, machine errors (that is, hardware faults) must also be contended with. Besides the failure of power or air-conditioning, and permanent damage to data media (for example, a disc head crash) or the computer itself, transients (the temporary malfunction of the computer hardware) are extremely troublesome. This type of error is treated in more detail in the next section.

Since the services of an operating system are required during the execution of user software, the errors in the operating system also contribute to an increased probability of failure of a user task. The more extensive, general and flexible an operating system is, the greater the number of errors that can be expected in it.

Hopkins (1970, p. 20) states, for example: 'We face a fantastic problem in big systems. For instance, in OS 360 we have about 1000 errors each release and this number seems reasonably constant.'

As well as operating system errors, arithmetic errors such as overflow, which only appear at run time, should be mentioned.

Transient Hardware Faults

The special treatment of transient hardware faults results from the fact that these faults are very often mistaken for software errors. Although according to Ball and Hardie (1969) in many technologies the probability of occurrence of this type of fault exceeds the probability of occurrence of a permanent hardware fault, there is little information in the literature on this class of fault. This is possibly explained by the fact that the interval, by definition short, during which the fault occurs is too short for the clear identification of the fault by the execution of a test program.

The cause of transient hardware faults may on the one hand be due to intermittent interference in either the power supply or physical environment of the computer (for example, shock); alternatively, it may be due to the gradual breakdown of a component. During an extensive simulation study (Ball and Hardie, 1969) of the characteristics of this type of fault, the following points emerged.

(1)   The control unit is more susceptible to transient faults than the arithmetic unit.

(2)   The probability that a fault that has occurred in the control unit will be immediately detected during the further execution of an instruction is an order of magnitude less than for a fault that has occurred in the arithmetic unit.

(3)   Transient faults are only of consequence when they last for more than one
      cycle time.

As already mentioned, the consequences of a transient fault are either
incorrect data or the incorrect flow of control. Since these symptoms are also
characteristic of software errors the wrong conclusion is often drawn as to the
cause of a system failure, especially when a checkout of the hardware by means
of a diagnostic program shows the hardware to be apparently fully functional.

Transient faults cause correspondingly more difficulties where there is
little error detection logic in the hardware (for example, memory parity checking).
This is especially true for the numerous mini-computer systems.

Although it has to be accepted that a part of the error statistics that
appear under the heading of 'unexplained errors' must be attributed to transient
errors, the view should not be taken that this type of error is synonymous with
unexplained system behaviour, especially during the development and commissioning of a software system. It should be possible to estimate the probability of
occurrence of these faults after long-term testing of the hardware. The possibility
of such faults should not, however, be neglected in the development of highly
reliable systems, since for such systems they may become the dominant cause of
failure.

Data-bank Errors

If a system processes numerous data items, a distinction must be made between
the case where the data may be treated as being external to the system, and the
case where the data forms an integral part of the system. In the first case a clear
separation between the input and output data exists. Should an error occur
during processing, then it is not particularly difficult to restart the computation,
that is, to re-initialise the system. At the end of the processing the output data
may be checked for plausibility (for example, check sums, number of records
processed, and so on) before it is used as input data for further processing. By
keeping archives of several generations of data it is possible to back-track several
processing steps.

A more complicated situation exists when the data must be treated as an
integral part of the system. In this case, in order to eliminate an error occurring
in the system, it is necessary to start from an error-free and precisely defined
state of the system. The definition of this state, however, represents a considerable
problem due to the quasi-continous changing nature of the stored data. Clearly,
all transactions that have been made since the system state was defined have to
be repeated. In such systems, data preparation may be better checked by the
immediate comparison of the input transaction with prestored data. However,
owing to the continually changing nature of the stored data, the checking of the
contents of files by means of plausibility tests or sum checks is more difficult
than in the first case discussed. In addition there are the increased complexities
of parallel processing.

The storage of an erroneous data element, therefore, cannot be discounted. Should this erroneous data element then be used as the input to a further transaction, the result of this transaction will also be in error.

This slow propagation of errors can lead to an erosion of the data bank, which in certain circumstances may only be detected after months have elapsed. At such a time, the necessary data and record of transactions required for the regeneration of the data will probably no longer be available in the archives. A regular inspection of the contents of a data bank is therefore essential.

To summarise, the more complicated it is to restore a defined state of a system after the occurrence of an error, the higher will be the cost of any error and consequently the reliability requirements on the system will increase. It is therefore good practice always to be aware of the significant advantages that are offered by a simple initialisation procedure for the complete system.

4 *Software Structure*

'And simplicity is the unavoidable price we must pay for reliability!'
C. A. R. Hoare (1975) p.533

The structure of an extensive system is decisive for the understanding and consequently for the perceived complexity of such a system. The complexity, however, has a decisive influence on the probability of an error being made in the design phase. Reliability can thus be increased by a clear and simple structure. Clear and simple in this context are related to the limited intellectual ability of the human brain. If a software system is difficult to understand, then it already contains the seeds of unreliability.

'If the intellectual effort required to understand and test a system increases more than linearly with the size of the system, we shall never be able to build reliable systems beyond a certain complexity.' (Brinch Hansen, 1973, p. 36.)

The structure of a system is a reduced representation of the system which still retains all the system characteristics that are relevant for the given purpose. Omitting all the fine details, the structure retains all the major features of the complete system. If it is not possible to find such a reduced representation, then the system does not contain any recognisable structure. If, on the other hand, it is possible to find such reduced representations of the system at various levels of abstraction, then the system is said to possess a hierarchy of structures. A software system may be represented in a number of forms (Parnas, 1972a), for example, as source program or as object program. Each form serves a specific purpose, for example, for human communication or execution by the machine. In changing from one form of representation to another (for example, by means of a compiler) the corresponding structure of the software may be considerably modified, or even substantially demolished. The following section deals primarily with the forms of representation of a software system that are intended for human communication. The structure of these forms of representation must take into account the idiosyncrasies and limits of comprehension of the human mind.

A characteristic of the human intellect is, on the one hand, the sequential thought process and, on the other, the fact that man can bear in mind only a very limited number of things simultaneously. To make his way through a complex world man has availed himself of the method of abstraction, the separation of a general form from concrete facts.

This general form may be treated as an elementary unit in the formulation of a number of building blocks which in turn lead to further building blocks. By the repeated use of the principle of abstraction, a hierarchical system is developed. A hierarchical system thus consists of a number of connected subsystems, which in turn are built from further hierarchies, and eventually from elementary units. It is important to realise that the term hierarchy used in the current context does not impose any constraints on the subsystems. No statement is made concerning the corresponding relationship among the subsystems. The special case of a distinct sub-order, as for example with the structure of a business organisation, is here designated as a formal hierarchy.

Simon (1962) states that in Nature many complex systems possess such a hierarchical structure. To support this statement he draws on a series of examples from various scientific disciplines, such as physics, astronomy, biology and sociology. The somewhat philosophical question as to the reason for the frequent occurence of such hierarchical structures is then posed. Whether structural hierarchies are a fundamental principle of nature or an artefact of human understanding is not relevant to the present discussion; they do, however, offer an appropriate means for the construction of artificial systems.

In a hierarchical system, a distinction has to be made between interactions inside the subsystems (intrasystem) and interactions between subsystems (that is, intersystem) (Simon, 1962). The stronger the intrasystem interactions (in comparison to the intersystem interactions), the more pronounced is the system structure and hence the easier it is to understand. Also important to the understanding of a hierarchy is its span. This means the number of subsystems which appear on the same level of the hierarchy. If the span is narrow then the hierarchy is said to be steep; otherwise it is said to be flat. The span of a hierarchy is determined by the ability of its components to support strong interaction. It is an important factor in understanding the relationships on any given level. Flat hierarchies are more difficult to analyse than steep ones.

These general remarks concerning the understanding of hierarchical systems may also be used in the simplification of modular software systems. In this context a module is taken to be synonymous with a subsystem. The complexity of such a software system may be reduced when the coupling between modules — the intermodule coupling — is reduced, and the internal (intramodule) coupling of the individual modules is increased.

4.1 INTERMODULE COUPLING

During the development of a software system, every effort must be made to keep the interconnections between the individual modules to a minimum. Primarily an interconnection is regarded as the transfer of control in the instruction space, the passing of parameters, or the common use of data fields in the data space. Parnas (1971) takes the term interconnection further, and postulates that it is any assumption made by one part of the system regarding the function of another. Should this assumption no longer be valid then an error will occur. To minimise interconnection Parnas suggests strict supervision of the information flow between the individual parts of a complex software system during its development. During the development of a part of a system only the absolutely necessary assumptions concerning the function of the remainder of the system may be made available. If a detailed knowledge of the internal construction of the remainder of the system is available, then the temptation to use this knowledge in building a module, and thereby increase the coupling to the remainder of the system, is very great.

Table 4.1 summarises the various types of coupling that can occur between modules (from Stevens *et al.*, 1974).

Table 4.1

Coupling	Interface complexity	Control transfer method	Method of communication
Loose	Simple, clear	To module via its name	Data
Tight	Complicated, confused	To internal element of module	Control changes by means of commands inside a module

Interface complexity includes all external data connections for a given module. If the module interface consists of a clear parameter transfer, then the external connections are substantially simpler than when a shared data field, such as the COMMON field in FORTRAN, is used. Often, in practice, too little attention is paid to the fact that the use of such shared data fields or control blocks results in tight coupling of many modules. In the event of an error, every single element of a shared data area can propagate secondary, and thus uncontrollable, effects. Often, because of such unnecessary connections to a shared data field, the coupling of the modules in such a system is much tighter than required to fulfil its function.

If the execution of a module is treated as a process (see section 2.2), then it makes sense to separate strictly the internal data of this process from the rest of the system. This leads, by means of a hierarchical construction of modules corresponding to the processes, to a natural organisation of data, which in turn leads to a minimum of data being handled on any given level, that is, only input and output data for the process. Parnas (1972a) suggests isolation of the knowledge about the physical representation of data from the rest of the system, by means of special data management modules which offer only logical data access. By this means many unnecessary assumptions regarding the physical representation of data elements are avoided, and the coupling between various system parts is reduced.

If the transfer of control can be made through a module name without reference to the physical location of the module, then the coupling is less complex than when the transfer is made through relative or absolute addressing.

Every module must communicate with its environment if it is to function as a component of the total system. The simplest way of implementing this is by means of data in parameter lists. If, however, the communication is by means of a special control transfer, or by accessing a specific code within the module, then the module is much more tightly coupled to its environment than it would be otherwise. The input data to a module that has been called may be of two types, either pure data or control information. Whereas the pure data is transformed in some predefined fashion, the control information indicates how the transformation is to be carried out. If the transfer of such control information is required then the calling module must be aware of the various options available in the module being called. This leads to additional coupling between the modules (Myers, 1973). Further coupling of a module with its environment exists when the communication is via an internal memory. This internal memory – the storing of data within a module, through various calling sequences – can have the effect that the results given by the module are no longer independent of the results from preceding computations, and therefore require further analysis. In such a case, the module is no longer independent of time.

The independence of a module is also destroyed when the module that has been called contains assumptions about the identity of the calling module.

4.2   INTRAMODULE COUPLING

In addition to the technique of reducing intermodule connections, an improved software system structure may be achieved by increasing the coupling within the various modules. The stronger the connections between the elements of a module, the greater the compactness of the module. Stevens *et al.* (1974), whose work has laid the foundation for the following section, suggest six levels of coupling, where the tightness of the coupling increases from level to level. These connections are

    incidental
    logical
    time-related
    communicative
    sequential
    functional.

An incidental connection means a connection is made where there is no obvious relationship between the elements of a module. This type of connection occurs, for example, when several completed sections of a program are arbitrarily concatenated to form a module. An incidental connection is the weakest of all connections and does not have any structure-enforcing properties.

The logical connection assumes the existence of certain logical relationships between the elements of a module. An example of a logical connection is the collection of all input and output data into a single program module. Since the collection is made on a logical basis and not on a functional basis – the actual input and output data may have vastly different characteristics – the logical connection often leads to weakly related program sections.

With the time-related connection, as well as there being a fixed logical similarity of function, there is also a time-dependent relationship, for example, the initialisation of a system. Often an initialisation module will contain the most diverse of functions connected logically and in a time-related sense.

A connection is said to be communicative when the individual parts of a module address the same input and output data, thereby achieving an already relatively high measure of coupling.

The sequential connection refers to the situation where the output data from one program section is used as the input data by the next program section. If a flow-chart is used to formulate a problem solution, then the extraction of certain parts of the chart to form a program module leads to the sequential connection of its elements. Since the extraction of parts of the solution does not necessarily lead to a self-contained function, the sequential connection is not as strong as the functional connection.

The functional connection is the strongest, and hence the most desirable, form of connection between the elements of a program module. With this type of connection all the elements of a module participate in the implementation of a single self-contained function; that is, the given input data is transformed into the desired output data. If, for example, it is necessary to provide a module with control information as well as pure data, then the module contains several functions. The functional connection contains major elements of the connections that we have already described and leads to a substantial consolidation of the structure of a software system.

The implementation of a self-contained function should use modules of a manageable size. It is generally accepted that a module is manageable if it contains about 50 executable statements and the source program listing requires no more than one page. When a module becomes too large, an attempt should be made to define self-contained sub-functions which can be implemented themselves as individual modules, and which in turn may eventually be accessed by other programs.

4.3 STRUCTURE AND EFFICIENCY

Well-defined structure and run-time efficiency are two desirable goals during system design. At first sight these two goals seem to be in contradiction. A well-defined structure means that, as far as possible, the various functions are implemented as independent modules. The calling of these individual modules during the execution of a program implies an additional management overhead (temporary storing of registers, return addresses, and so on) which reduces the system efficiency. In addition, the structuring of a system can lead to an increased expenditure of space, since many modules may contain identical short sequences of instructions.

As a result of the conflict between structure and efficiency, in many software projects the structure has been sacrificed to achieve an apparent increase in efficiency. It is assumed that the direct cross-coupling of control by the use of common code sequences and data fields, and the construction of the flattest possible structure with few subprogram calls, will lead to a substantial increase in efficiency. The complexity will certainly increase, owing to the increased connectivity, as will the difficulty of achieving other objectives such as reliability, maintainability and adaptability. In practice, only in a few software projects can the real performance bottlenecks be determined in advance during the design phase, since at that time only approximate data concerning the use and the run-time behaviour of the system are available. Experience shows (for example, Knuth, 1971 and 1974) that the greatest part of the run-time, for programs that are not heavily input/output dependent, is concentrated within a small portion of the source text. If, once the system has become operational, information of the above nature becomes known, then it is possible without too much difficulty to adjust the system better to is actual application. A major increase in efficiency may only be achieved by the analysis of the data flow as a whole. These changes may only be made, however, when the coupling of the individual parts of the system is obvious and may be controlled, that is, when the system has a clear structure. Hopkins (1970, p. 101) states: 'There will be less attention to operations that result in improvements in the 10 per cent range and more to those that yield orders of magnitude improvement.'

A certain amount of ambiguity between understandable structure and run-time efficiency undoubtedly exists. It is not nearly as great as is widely assumed. In the previous section it was stated that steep hierarchies are easier to understand and analyse than flat hierarchies. On the other hand, the overhead inherent in steep structure due to subprogram calls is greater. Finding a workable compromise is one of the tasks to be carried out during system design. It is, nevertheless, not advisable to sacrifice the structure, for reasons of efficiency which may, up to this point, be unclear and therefore of secondary importance. Otherwise, the result will be increased unreliability of the product. A subsequent increase in reliability is much more difficult to achieve than an increase in efficiency. An inefficient software product can often be used to advantage before its optimisation. This is seldom the case with an unreliable product.

Finally it should be noted that, based on present developments in the computer hardware field, extremes of optimisation, such as the saving of individual instructions and storage locations, should be avoided, if only on the grounds of cost (figure 4.1).

If a software system can only be implemented by the use of such extreme optimisation measures, then the choice of the original hardware configuration was incorrect.

On the other hand, it should not be assumed that there are almost unlimited hardware resources available. Each additional hardware resource has associated

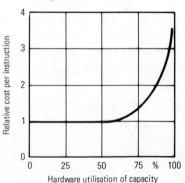

Figure 4.1 Relationship between programming costs and utilisation of hardware capacity (Williman and Donnel, 1970)

with it a penalty, in terms of (hardware) unreliability, which must be considered when assessing the overall system. It remains for the system designer to weigh up the various factors involved and find an acceptable middle way.

4.4 THE DESCRIPTION OF A SYSTEM

The understanding of a system is very strongly dependent on the description chosen. In the case of software, three descriptions with differing emphases may be used, these being respectively data-oriented, process-oriented and program-oriented.

Central to the data-oriented description are the various states that the data can take during the course of a computation.

In the foreground of the process-oriented description are the dynamics of the data transformations. Their importance derives from the fact that this form of description comes closest to the way in which a digital computer functions. Man, however, is only in a position to follow sequential processes, and then, mostly, when there are no real-time considerations to be taken into account. Despite this, in a number of cases the characteristics of a system, especially the interaction of several parallel running processes, only become clear after the process-oriented description has been analysed.

Finally the program-oriented description deals with the individual programs. Since every complete software system must have this type of description — the actual sequence of instructions carried out by the computer is laid down in the program itself — this is the most widespread form of software system representation. To demonstrate the function of a system the program-oriented description is not as suitable as either the process-oriented or data-oriented description.

The structure of a system is greatly influenced by the type of description chosen to represent the system during its development. The program-oriented description leads ultimately to a program-oriented design — the individual programs are at the focal point — whereas the process and data-oriented descriptions lead to a data-oriented design – the data transformations (processes) and the attendant data structures (input and output data) are at the centre of the design.

A comparison of these two design techniques shows that, from a reliability point of view, data orientation is to be preferred to program orientation (Schwartz, 1970, p. 134)

If a system is built around the relevant data, it is possible, at any time, to make a clear and unambiguous statement about the state of the system.

Through the exact definition of the data associated with each level of abstraction, a clearly arranged subdivision of the system can be obtained.

In the initial phase of a system design, the system description may be reduced to a definition of the input and output data for the individual processes. The logical structure of the data can be made to be independent of the actual algorithms chosen and the physical representation of the data; furthermore this leads to well-defined interfaces. If, for example, an algorithm or input/ output device has to be changed, then only the logical data interfaces have to be checked.

The verification of a system is made considerably easier. Debugging aids can be built around the data, thus allowing easier test automation.

If the data contains intentional redundancy, then it is possible to check system integrity while the system is running. For example, gross errors may be detected by checking the range of certain key variables or by some other simple plausibility tests.

The recovery of a system after an error is made considerably easier.

The development of a data-oriented system starts with the definition of the logical data elements. As soon as this phase has been defined, a start may be made on the data transformation processes. If the physical construction of the data is separated from the logical data structure by means of data management modules (Parnas, 1972a; Geschke and Mitchell, 1975), then the construction of the physical data may be changed without having to change all the modules that use the logical data sets. Unfortunately, existing programming languages are not best suited to data-oriented system design. It would have been advantageous if a separation had been made between physical data definition and logical data processing.

However, despite this it is possible to design data-oriented systems with present day programming languages. Michael Jackson has developed a data-oriented design methodology which is being used in the commercial data-processing environment, using COBOL. The following three-step procedure is the foundation of his design technique (Jackson, 1975, p. 43)

'(i)   consider the problem environment and record our understanding of it by defining structures of the data to be processed;

(ii)   form a program structure based on the data structures;

(iii) define the task to be performed in terms of the elementary operations available, and allocate each of those operations to suitable components of the program structure.'

5 *Functional Specification*

The functional specification defines the function of a planned system from the point of view of the user, and thereby provides a link between the user and the system designer. The user should ascertain whether on the basis of the functional specification provides a basis for the design and implementation. His main requirements on the specification are completeness and consistency. All subsequent specification provides a basis for the design and implementation. The main requisites for the specification are completeness and consistency. All subsequent statements regarding the correctness of a particular implementation must take the specification as a reference norm. If it is not complete or contains inconsistencies then no decision can be made as to whether the system development was correct or not.

The preparation of a complete and unambiguous specification, which conforms with the intentions of the user, is one of the most difficult tasks involved in the development of an extensive system. The analysis of software errors shows that from one-third to one-half of all errors can be attributed to an incomplete, inconsistent, or false specification (see section 3.3).

The parts of the system that have been specified in a quick and superficial way are usually those that contain the most logical errors. According to Boehm (1974) any additional effort expended during the specification stage gives more than a two-fold return in labour saving during the coding, testing and integration phases. The specification is not only of great importance from the point of view of reliability, but also from the point of view of project management. As the first major document in the system development it represents the point of departure from which progress may be monitored.

5.1 CONTENT

A good functional specification contains all necessary statements regarding the desired function of the system, and nothing more. 'There is also an abstraction involved in naming an operation and using it on account of "what it does" while completely disregarding "how it works" ' (Dijkstra, 1972b, p. 111). Each additional statement has a number of adverse effects; it obscures the function of the system, while burdening the user with unimportant detail, and it restricts the flexibility of the later development. The concentration on the function – the 'what' (the logical relationships) – and not on the physical realisation – the 'how' – gives the system developer the maximum amount of freedom during the implementation phase, and allows for the optimal combined use of hardware and software during the development. This approach, while reducing the extent and complexity of the specification, can prove to be most difficult in practice.

A good specification may always be recognised from its clear and distinct organisation. While being virtually free of specialised computer jargon, it should draw the user's attention to the important system functions.

Description of the System Functions

This is the essential part of the specification. Starting with the desired outputs, the required inputs and the coupling between the inputs and outputs should be described. Since the user may only have a limited ability to follow a formal terminology, a means of representation must be chosen that is familiar to the user from his everyday environment.

Liskov and Zilles (1975) advocate that a formal representation should always be used, thus allowing for possibly mechanised processing of the specification. Since in some cases the use of a program is based solely on the functional specification, under such circumstances it is irrelevant whether this specification conforms to the original customer's intentions or not.

One solution to this problem is to draw up two specifications, one suitable for the customer which is mostly verbal, and the other a formal description which can be a starting point for the system development (Rault, 1973). However, in such a case it is essential for these two specifications to be consistent.

It is particularly important that the functional specification contains a description of the environment in which the new system is to operate, and a definition of the interface between the system and this environment. The environment description should contain

the economic incentives for the installation of the system
the organisational situation
the human operators, their role and qualification
the physical characteristics of the environment
the maintenance organisation for hardware and software.

The interface definition should include

the man-machine interface including the dialogues and the reporting system
the planned operating procedures
the hardware interface to conventional electronic equipment (if any).

Such a clear definition of the interface between the planned system and its environment is necessary in order to define exactly the extent of the system on the one hand and to enable the user to make early provisions for the start up of the system on the other hand.

Data Description

The functional specification must also contain a description of the upper and lower limits of the input and output data. Only then is it possible to detect errors in the input data and check the plausibility of the results. The plausible range of the data at specific points in the computation should also be given so that reasonableness checks can be performed during the computation as well. Since the digital representation and manipulation of real values is rarely exact, the result of a computation with real numbers will contain certain errors. The functional specification must state the permissible range of this error band so that there are no errors due to loss of significance in a particular application.

Time and Throughput Requirements

The volume of input data that the system is expected to handle is a very important parameter for the system design. In real-time systems it is good practice also to specify the distribution of the input data over time and to relate this distribution to the expected response time of the system.

Reliability Requirements

Developing a reliable system means that in every phase of the development each possible error source is analysed and suitable measures for the prevention of such errors or the minimisation of their effect are taken. For this purpose it is necessary to make a list of possible error sources and of critical error effects. The error source list should contain possible error sources and the associated probabilities of their occurence in the given application, for example, environmental disturbances, input errors by unqualified operators, hardware failures of key components, etc. The error effect list should describe the effect of an error in the primary system functions (see section 3.2). It should be specified which level of degraded performance of the system is still sufficient for the user to maintain a minimum level of service in case an error has occurred.

In particularly critical situations it may be necessary to maintain essential system functions by means of a simple emergency standby system. The functional specification must contain a description of this standby system so that a smooth switchover between the normal and emergency operation (and vice versa) may be designed during the system development.

Acceptance Criteria

The formulation of quantitative acceptance criteria by which the performance of the completed system can be measured, is particularly important. There should be an explicit acceptance criterion for each individual requirement of the system. If it is not possible to find such a quantitative criterion for a particular required function, there are grounds for assuming that the user is uncertain as to the worth and meaning of the requirement (Gibson and Railing, 1971).

5.2 CHANGES AND MODIFICATIONS

To what extent requests for changes that effect the specification should be considered during the system development is in practice an especially delicate subject. As a consequence of further thought about the new system, the user may increase the depth of his understanding and change his requirements. Real world problems are usually not well defined, but ill structured. 'In real life there is not a single static, well-defined problem but a constantly changing problem whose definition is being altered by information that actors recover from memory and by other information from the environment's response to actions taken.' (Simon, 1971, p. I.264.)

On the other hand, changes to the functional specification can have the following effects on the system development (Gibson and Railing, 1971)

    destruction of the system structure and hence the quality
    increased personnel costs
    additional errors
    increased effort in system verification
    deterioration in the motivation of personnel.

If no changes are made because of the above considerations, it may become necessary for an extensive rewrite of the system after it becomes operational. Boehm (1974) mentions that large software projects have been completely abandoned because they did not conform to the user's requirements. In other cases a 95 per cent rewrite of the code was necessary. The most sensible solution is a scrupulous preparation of the specification in conjunction with the user, and the limitation of subsequent changes to an absolute minimum (see also section 12.3). The preparation of the functional specification for a complex system is, to some extent, an iterative process. If a large labour force is involved in this process, it is essential to document fully each iteration. Finally, the user must accept the content of the functional specification without any reservation.

5.3 SPECIFICATION AIDS

A review of how the effort in a software project is distributed into the various development phases, shows that approximately 20 per cent of the total effort is devoted to the preparation of the functional specification — the so-called logical system design (Cougar, 1973) — and the percentage has been growing rapidly in recent years. This not inconsiderable task — it can, for example, be greater than that required in the actual coding — has led to the development of a number of methods and mechanised aids for the preparation of the functional specification. The approach has been two-fold, dealing on the one hand with verbal descriptions and on the other with formal specification languages. These techniques help in the derivation of a complete and unambiguous specification and, hence, an increased reliability.

The Systems Organisation Plan (SOP), as the first complete technique for systems analysis, was introduced by IBM in 1961 (IBM, 1961). SOP is a comprehensive design method for the understanding and analysis of the information requirements of a complete organisation. After the initial collection of data relating to the existing manual system, the next step is preparation of a specification for the automatic data processing and an investigation of its probable impact on the organisation. For each phase of the system analysis a comprehensive set of forms is maintained, which are designed to help the analyst in a systematic and complete compilation of all requirements.

A similar method is offered by the ARDI-method (Analysis, Requirement Determination, Design and Development, Implementation and Evaluation), introduced by Hartmann *et al.* in 1968.

Characteristic for both methods is the mainly verbal description of the system. Herein, perhaps, lies the reason for the limited acceptance of these otherwise excellent systems analysis methods.

In recent years semigraphical notations for systems analysis have replaced the purely verbal description. One of these methods, HIPO (Hierarchy, Input, Process and Output), has gained wide acceptance. The functional specification is created by naming the basic functions which have to be performed and decomposing them into hierarchically ordered sub-functions. Each function in the hierarchy is represented as a box and can be described within that box as a verb (action) and an object (data affected). The verb—object format thus names as well as describes the function. An input—process—output (IPO) diagram is associated with each box.

A step further away from verbal specification is the Structured Analysis and Design Technique (SADT) developed by SOFTECH (Ross and Shoman, 1977). The notation of SADT is a diagramming language, which describes the relationship between objects and activities. With this notation it is possible to model complex systems from different viewpoints. The diagrams produced under SADT do show a certain aspect of a system at a certain level of detail. The amount of information which may be put on a SADT diagram is strictly controlled, so that diagrams are not overloaded.

In addition to this diagramming language SADT also specifies a set of procedures for a disciplined approach towards the systems analysis process. The working relationship between the systems analyst and the user, the documentation and filing of all project reports is regulated in detail. A disadvantage of this methodology lies in the strictly manual evaluation of the collected information, at least at the moment.

This disadvantage was overcome in the third generation of systems analysis techniques. Here an attempt is made to get the computer itself to help with the analysis. Automatic decision tables – processors – and the Time Automated Grid (TAG) were the first comprehensive systems of this type (Head, 1971). Starting with the desired system outputs, the TAG indicates when each input is required. Redundant or missing data fields can be detected and corrected. When the input and output data have been defined, a further iteration step gives the required files and the data flow through the system. In addition TAG can produce a list of all data fields, names and the time relationships between the data inputs, system resident data and the required outputs. With these as a basis the systems analyst is able to define an optimal file structure.

The methods thus far mentioned have all attempted to automate various aspects of the systems analysis. ISDOS (Information System Design and Optimisation System) integrates all the stages of systems development, from the definition of the system specification to the development of the completed system (Teichreow and Hershey, 1977). Although this system is still in development, part of ISDOS is operational.

The ISDOS developers started with the assumption that it is almost impossible to write an 'absolutely correct' functional specification. It is therefore desirable to automate (and thus accelerate and simplify) the development processes themselves, so that changes to the specification can be quickly processed to produce a new version of the system. It is essential with such a system to separate the user's requirement (the functional specification) from the decision as to how these requirements will be implemented. By using a special purpose language the 'Problem Statement Language' (PSL) the analyst can formulate the system function in a form that can be directly read by the machine, without having to revert to the procedure-oriented languages which up until now have been available. This machine-legible form of 'Problem Statement', which is the 'what' as opposed to the 'how', is processed automatically in ISDOS by the 'Problem Statement Analyser'. This produces the following

a comprehensive data dictionary, and a list of all functions
a static network analysis, so that the completeness and the consistency of the relationships can be checked
a dynamic analysis, so that the time relationships can be checked.

The result of this first step is a problem definition which is partly in machine-legible form. It is also planned to support the actual system development by means of further ISDOS modules.

An excellent survey of other systems analysis and design methods that are available can be found in Peters, 1978.

6 Reliability and System Design

The reliability of an extensive software system is essentially determined during the design stage. If the system design is poor, that is, without understandable structure, then in the majority of cases it is not possible to provide a highly reliable product by later corrections. If, on the other hand, more effort is put into the elimination of errors during the design phase, then considerable savings will be made during later debugging. In this chapter, the prevention of system design errors is investigated. In the first section the corner-stone of all software systems, the sequential process, is analysed in detail. When a number of processes run quasi-simultaneously, a number of new problems and sources for error appear; these are dealt with in the subsequent section. In the final section of the chapter, programming is considered from the point of view of reliability.

6.1 SEQUENTIAL PROCESSES

The term 'process' as the dynamic counterpart of the static term 'program' has already been introduced earlier (section 2.2). The distinction between the terms 'process', 'action sequence' and 'computation' lies in the abstraction made from the state of the data and the flow of control. Only the input, output and internal variables are of interest at the abstraction level of the process. A sequential process is present when all the actions of the process logically follow one another.

The concept of the sequential process is of fundamental importance to the design of a software system. It is the natural way in which the human mind performs the rational analysis of a problem; it is also the way in which information processing machines operate. The sequential process represents a fundamental building block in bridging the gap between the functional specification and the operation of the computer. This is, however, exactly the problem of system development.

Every program is developed with the intention of generating a process which performs the desired transformation of the input data. The clearer the relationship between a program and the corresponding processes, the easier it will be to understand the system.

Structured Programming

In the last few years a special design technique, structured programming, has been developed with the object of bringing out, in the clearest and most understandable way, the relationship between the program text and the corresponding processes. The term 'structured programming' was introduced by Dijkstra in 1972 and more exactly defined by Mills in 1972 in 'Mathematical Foundations of Structured Programming'. Subsequently, however, the term has been used in so many contexts that the meaning has become more general and less clear. Denning (1974, p. 6) has asked, 'But what is "structured programming"? The following seem to encompass most of the impressions people seem to have of it

(1)   It is a return to common sense, an awakening to the realisation that we are about to choke on the myriad of "features" and "options" we have been building into languages and systems.
(2)   It is the general method by which our leading programmers program.
(3)   It is programming without the use of GOTO statements.
(4)   It is the process of controlling the number of interactions between a given local task or block and its environment so that the number of interactions is some linear function of some parameter or parameters of the task or block.
(5)   It is top down programming.'

So that the differences in interpretation of the term 'structured programming' can be avoided, in what follows it will be taken in the sense described by Mills (1972, p. 4): '*Structured programming* ... identifies the programming process with a step by step expansion of mathematical functions into structures of logical connectives and subfunctions, carried out until the derived subfunctions can be directly realised in the programming language being used.'

Starting from the functional specification a software system is designed step by step from the outside inwards. Each step in the development leads to the production of a so-called segment, which may be directly implemented as a sequence of instruction in the language being used, or refers to further subordinate segments. As soon as all segments have been completed, then the complete system has been developed. In order to guarantee the manageability and understandability of the individual segments, each segment should be made as independent of the rest of the system as possible. This means that there should be only one entry point and one exit; the segment should not produce side effects, and should contain a limited number (approximately 50 executable) source level instructions.

Since the program is a step-by-step development from the functional specification, it is not necessary to implement unconditional branching (the GOTO instruction). Experience has shown that unconditional branching often leads to programs that are difficult to follow, and makes the relationships between the program and the process difficult to ascertain (Dijkstra, 1968). This avoidance of the GOTO does not, however, impose any serious restrictions on the programmer. According to a theorem by Böhm and Jacopini (1966), it is possible to take any given program in the form of a flow diagram with a single start and single end point, and mechanically translate it into an equivalent program that contains only the three control elements 'IF THEN ELSE', 'DO WHILE' and sequencing (figure 6.1). These three control elements each have only one start and one end point, and thus comply with the requirements for the production of a structured program. While the purely mechanical translation does indeed lead to a program free of the GOTO, it does not necessarily mean that this produces a structured program in the sense described above.

The restriction of the number of statements and the clear control flow mean that each segment of a structured program is suited to human powers of comprehension. Since the relationships between the program text and the process can easily be visualised, the probability of errors during system development is greatly reduced by the use of structured programming.

How does structured programming relate to the modular systems development technique? Can a segment of a structured program be equated with a module? It is certainly necessary to define the term 'MODULE' more exactly, since it also has been used in varying contexts.

Modularity

In many areas of engineering a range of systems is constructed from a limited number of components – the modules. With modular programming an attempt is made to use this technique for the development of software systems. With a limited number of standardised software components it should be possible to

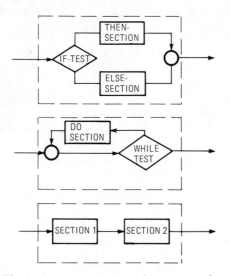

Figure 6.1 The basic components used in structural programming

build a large number of different systems. Perhaps the best way to describe modular programming is by the enumeration of its characteristics, as follows.

(1)   A module may be characterised by its function, by the source language being used, as well as by its expected performance related to the performance of the overall system.

(2)   The interface of a module to the rest of the system should be laid down in the simplest possible terms.

(3)   A program module should possess only one start and one end point within the control flow. Instructions within the module may not be altered during execution (Kopetz, 1974).

(4)   A module should be kept as general as possible, to allow for its use in as many contexts as possible.

(5)   It should be possible to prove the correctness of a module without reference to its context (Dennis, 1973).

(6)   It should be possible to link several modules together without a precise knowledge of their internal operation (Parnas, 1972b).

(7)   Modularity is more a property of the language level than a problem solution (Dennis, 1973).

(8)   The connectivity of different modules is determined by the assumptions that the individual modules make about each other. An individual module may only be changed as long as these assumptions remain constant (Parnas, 1971).

In many discussions the rules of modularity are taken as a subset of the rules of structured programming.[1]

If, however, a deeper analysis is made of the characteristics of structured and modular programming as described here, then, despite the many similarities between the two design techniques, distinct differences emerge.

(1)   The individual segments of a structured program are developed completely independently of one another. Each segment may be treated in quasi-isolation. In contrast to this, with modular programming the attempt is made to make each module as general as possible in order to render it widely applicable.

(2)   The segments of a structured program are related to each other through an ordered hierarchy. In comparison there is usually no such ordered relationship between individual modules.

(3)   The subdivision of a system into a formally ordered hierarchy of segments is determined by the problem definition, whereas a module is treated as an extension of the function of the language, in order to provide a tool in the solution of the problem.

---

1   See, for example, Martin, 1974, p. 665: 'In particular, the method of Structured Programming encourages top-down analysis of problems or the development of algorithms by stepwise refinement. Programs developed in this manner are automatically modular; hence structured programming provides a systematic way of modularising.'

The difference between structured and modular programming becomes more marked with larger systems. Whereas during modular programming an attempt is made to collect related functions into a generalised module, during structured programming, abiding by the rules described above, all the functions are realised as completely independent segments in parallel. This gives rise to a danger of duplication of work, which has led to the concept of the layered hierarchy being introduced.[1]

A complex system cannot be developed linearly, it has to be the result of a number of iterations (Zurcher and Randell, 1968; Woodger, 1971). It would appear reasonable to make a distinction between the actual system development and the preparation of the necessary tools required for the development.

The actual system development should follow the rules of structured programming. After laying out a complete and consistent specification, the system is resolved into a number of hierarchically ordered segments. As soon as this resolution is complete, it has to be determined what data transformations, in addition to those already implemented in the language being used, would simplify the system implementation. After the function of these new instructions has been defined, these new software tools are developed on a bottom-up basis. Then these tools are used during a repeated top-down analysis of the complete system, which must lead to a simplification of the system outlay. This iterative procedure is repeated until the overall structure can be seen as a combination of generalised software tools (or modules) forming a structured program.

The software tools stand outside the hierarchy of the structured program. They should be equated with the elementary instructions of the language being used, the use of which is not restricted by any kind of problem-specific ordering relation. If it is necessary to structure the tools themselves, then the internal structure of these tools has no relationship to the actual system structure.

It is advisable to distinguish between simple and complex tools during their development. A simple tool may be recognised from the fact that there is no internal storage of data between calls. Repeated calls achieve extensive, but independent, data transformations. Brinch Hansen (1973a) uses the term 'functional' to describe this property of simple tools.

Complex tools possess an internal memory, which is not re-initialised with every call. Thus the function of such a tool is directly dependent on the previous usage. This dependence on preceding calls may, in some cases, be desired for the solution of tasks that lie outside the scope of structured programming (for example, the time-overlapped use of resources by several parallel processes).

If such a distinction is made between modules and segments, then it is possible to combine the advantages of structured programming (clear structure) with those of modular programming (efficient use of the available resources).

---

1 cf. Dijkstra, 1972a, p. 50: 'The picture of a layered hierarchy of machines provides a counterpoise to one of the dangers evoked by ruthless application of the principles "Divide and Rule" viz. that different components are programmed so independently of each other that duplication of work (or worse) takes place.'

6.2   PARALLEL PROCESSES

In many cases it is required to solve a number of tasks simultaneously. This necessity may arise from efficiency considerations or from the dictates of the problem being considered. If a process is held up awaiting some external event, it is often expedient to release certain resources, such as the CPU, from the current process, and perform other tasks in the meantime (multiprogramming). On the other hand it may be necessary to split the given problem into a number of subprograms which may be processed quasi-simultaneously using different resources (multiprocessing), thereby easing the real-time constraint of the problem solution.

Two processes are said to run in parallel when they overlap in time, that is, when more than one process is to be found between its start and end point at a given time interval. It is irrelevant whether the individual actions of the parallel processes are executed simultaneously as in multiprocessing, or sequentially as in multiprogramming. In neither case can any statement be made concerning the progress of the parallel running processes relative to one another. This uncertainty regarding the relative progress leads to the by no means trivial problems of parallel processing.

The term parallel processing is only relevant on a given level of abstraction. Thus a certain process may be classified as being sequential or as parallel depending on how it is regarded. An obvious example is multiprogramming with a single CPU. As far as the user is concerned the user programs run sequentially. He is not aware of the fact that in the computer several programs can be processed simultaneously. From the point of view of the operating system, several user programs run simultaneously, that is, in parallel. Finally with reference to the CPU the processing proceeds again as a strictly sequential series of instructions. The switching over from one process to another cannot be distinguished from the execution of an instruction within a process on this level. Similar situations often exist in the relationship between hardware and software. A machine instruction may be executed in parallel by the hardware, although this fact may be completely concealed from the software.

Parallel processes are of particular significance to reliability, when an attempt is made to increase the hardware reliability by using several identical hardware components. In the event of the malfunction of one of these components in such a system, the important functions may be taken over by the remaining operational components. This attempt at increased reliability of the hardware will only be completely successful if the interdependencies of the parallel processes are kept completely under control. In many real-time systems a large number of errors that are difficult to locate can be traced back to the neglect of these interdependencies. Typical examples are the overwriting of data areas, or the deadlock problem.

Common to all of these errors is a characteristic time relationship of certain events. Since it is nearly impossible to repeat all time-related events in a complex real-time system, it is often only with great difficulty that these errors can be reproduced.

The great effort required for the identification and elimination of these errors, and the attendant negative influence on reliability can only be minimised when the unintended influences of parallel processes are excluded on theoretical grounds.

In developing a system with parallel processing, the first task is the specification of the individual sequential processes. First, the independence of these individual processes is established. From these independent sequential processes, a step-by-step and controlled introduction of the inter-process relationships is carried out.

In what follows it is assumed that during the running of parallel processes all requirements for additional resources are met. Under such circumstances a sufficient condition for the independence of two processes P_1 and P_2 is that neither output area overlaps the other, nor is there any overlapping of either process input area with the output area of the other process (Coffman and Denning, 1973, p. 38).

This condition may be extended to cover the independence of a number of parallel processes. The independence of parallel processes is not affected when these processes use common input variables, assuming that none of the variables is modified by the processes.

In practice, resources are limited and a certain amount of communication between parallel processes is required. In what now follows it is assumed that the communication between parallel processes is restricted to the exchange of information.

When individual processes compete for the same resources, and thus indirectly influence one another, this is known as implicit coupling. If a given process requires resources without which it cannot proceed, and if these resources cannot be reallocated, then this can lead to a situation where all available resources have been allocated to the various parallel processes in such a way that no process has sufficient resources to proceed. This in turn leads to the blocking of parts of the system, or even the whole system. This coupling is known as implicit, since it lies beyond the control of any individual process; it is also called deadlock.

Coupling that is introduced to allow communication between individual processes is know as explicit coupling. If the individual processes exchange information — and a process can only proceed when it has received information that it is awaiting — a situation can arise where all processes are awaiting some piece of information before proceeding to produce further information, the lack of which is preventing the transmission of the original piece of information. In such a case, this will lead to the system coming to a complete standstill (Holt, 1971).

Implicit and explicit coupling thus impose certain restrictions on the parallel processing. It is therefore necessary to perform the resource allocation in such a manner that the given allocation criteria (for example, short response time, or high utilisation of resources) are considered under the condition that no standstill of the system (deadlock) can occur.

Deadlock

In the following it is assumed that every process, given sole access to all the system resources, will proceed unimpeded to its end point. Then the situation known as deadlock will occur when the system comes to a standstill due to coupling between processes. Coffman *et al.* (1971 p. 70) give the following necessary conditions for deadlock due to implicit coupling.

'(1)   Tasks claim exclusive control of the resources they require ("mutual exclusion" condition).
(2)   Tasks hold resources already allocated to them while waiting for additional resources ("wait for" condition).
(3)   Resources cannot be forcibly removed from the tasks holding them until the resources are used to completion ("no pre-emption" condition).
(4)   A circular chain of tasks exists, such that each task holds one or more resources that are being requested by the next task in the chain ("circular wait" condition).'

There are a number of strategies that can be used to avoid deadlock. It is sufficient to prevent the occurrence of any one of the above conditions in all circumstances, so that the occurrence of deadlock is impossible. The 'wait for' condition may be prevented by the rule that a process be allocated all the resources it requires to reach its end point, simultaneously. This, however, leads to very poor utilisation of the individual resources. An improved utilisation of resources may be achieved by adopting the strategy suggested by Havender (1968). This strategy entails assigning a cost to each resource, allocating them on a cheapest first basis. This ensures that at least one process has all the resources it requires for termination (prevention of 'circular wait' condition), and the demands on expensive resources are of short duration. This is the strategy adopted by the IBM operating system.

Another strategy for the avoidance of deadlock is to check each request for a re-allocation of system resources and determine if the new state of the system can lead to a deadlock. With this strategy a higher utilisation of the individual resources can be achieved. There is, however, the possibility that the execution of the algorithm which checks the new system state requires more effort than that gained from the increased resource utilisation. This can be particularly serious in the case of an approaching deadlock. Fontao (1972) reports a case where a system was slowed down by a factor of 10^4 due to the checking algorithm, which to all intents and purposes can itself be considered to constitute a deadlock.

Synchronisation

The explicit coupling of two processes that run in parallel results from the use of common resources, such as core store locations which both processes can access in order to exchange information. As one process builds up such information, there may exist a critical time interval during which the other process may not alter the information. As an example, consider the instruction sequence read—modify—write, during which no other process may write to the storage location being used since it will be immediately overwritten and the result lost. During development it must be ensured that during such critical time intervals only one process has access to common resources. The section of program that is being executed during this critical interval is known as the critical section, and the common resources from which the processes are to be prohibited as the critical region (figure 6.2). The problem discussed here is known in the literature as 'mutual exclusion'. Every solution to the mutual exclusion problem requires a synchronisation of the individual processes. The difficulty in solving this problem comes in the determination of minimal synchronisation conditions that are relevant to the requirements of the critical region. Even if they can be applied, trivial solutions such as the sequential execution of the processes are of little value.

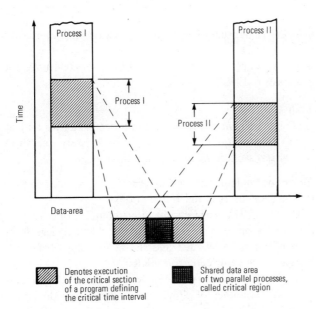

Figure 6.2 Relationship between critical section, critical time interval and critical region. If the critical sections of both processes overlap in time then an unintended side effect can arise

Brinch Hansen (1973a, p. 84) states that any realistic solution to the 'mutual exclusion' problem must satisfy the following criteria.

(1)   When a process wishes to enter a critical region, it will be enabled to do so within a finite time
(2)   At most, one process at a time can be inside a critical region.
(3)   A process remains inside a critical region for a finite time only.

If this last condition is not fulfilled – for example, one of the processes fails during the critical interval – a blocking of further processes that use the critical region may result. From a reliability point of view the critical time interval (that is, the critical sections of the programs) and the critical region should be kept as small as possible.

Dijkstra (1968b), referring to an example of the difficulty of the realisation of critical sections, suggests the introduction of two new elementary operations, which operate on two special integer variables known as the semaphore variables.

These two elementary operations are

$P(S): S \leftarrow S - 1$
    IF $S = 0$ THEN enter the critical section
        ELSE wait
$V(S): S \leftarrow S + 1$
    IF $S < 1$ THEN activate waiting process
        ELSE finish

The execution of these elementary processes may not, of course, be interrupted.

The simplest implementation of a critical section using the P and V operators appears as follows.

Initialisation $S \leftarrow 1$
$P(S)$ Postponement, if critical region is occupied by a critical section
$V(S)$ Critical region is free, possibly it is necessary to activate the
    critical section of the next waiting process

Thus the problem of implementing a critical section is reduced to the problem of implementing the elementary P and V operations.

Brinch Hansen (1972) suggests the direct coupling of critical sections with the critical regions (common variables) on a higher language level. Thus the semaphore variables can be avoided and the relationships between the critical sections and regions can be directly formulated.

An example of a critical region of a system is the on-line data bank, which may be altered by a number of simultaneous users. In order to allow parallel processing of the data bank, it is expedient to limit the critical region which exists at any time to individual data fields or records. Although this may be achieved by using the semaphore variables, the previously suggested Brinch Hansen coupling of the critical sections and regions is more suitable.

Another method of solving the problem of synchronisation is by the aid of monitors. A monitor can be considered as a data structure and a set of meaningful operations on that data structure. These operations can be accessed by the different parallel processes but can only be executed sequentially. If two processes want to execute a monitor operation at the same time, one is delayed until the other one has released the monitor (Hoare, 1974). A monitor protects the critical region in the data domain and ensures that only one parallel process can work on these data at any given time. However, the execution of the parallel processes can be delayed at the point of the monitor call. This can lead to serious problems in real-time situations.

In order to ensure software reliability, it is often advisable to proceed with a more restricted development than is perhaps theoretically necessary. This is especially so with parallel processes which are driven by asynchronous interrupts. The time relationships for such processes are random, the run-time environments are normally not protected (Wirth, 1969), and hence their interdependencies are particularly difficult to check exactly. Furthermore there is often a considerable risk of a spurious interrupt not being detected in the hardware. Therefore, if one has the choice, one should opt for the cyclic execution of tasks in preference to the interrupt driven execution of tasks.

6.3 PROGRAMMING STYLE

Next to a well-conceived structure, programming style has a decided effect on the comprehensibility of a software system. There are, of course, many ways in which a program may be written so that the required data transformations are performed. It is the individual programming style that finally decides which alternatives are chosen and whether the program looks clear or confused. Programming style determines the readability and thereby also the complexity. The relationship between reliability and complexity has already frequently been referred to. The most important rule of programming style requires that a program be simple, clear and manageable. The programming language being used plays an important role in determining the individual style.

The main consideration of any programming language should be comprehensibility and clear terminology. The following language attributes help in achieving this goal (Zilles, 1974, p. 21)

(1) the possibility for abstraction
(2) uniformity of language rules
(3) support of the semantics through the syntax
(4) few possibilities for error
(5) the language terminology should suit the application
(6) no unnecessary synonyms.

The following sections describe some additional rules of programming style (cf. Kernighan and Plauger, 1974a).

Physical Layout

The first impression of a program is given by its physical layout. The visual organisation of the program text using separating lines and indentation has a very positive effect on program readability. Weissmann (1974, p. 75) determined during an empirical investigation that the comprehensibility of a program has a significant dependence on its visual layout.

Nomenclatures

The choice of variable names is also important to readability. While variable names should be chosen from a mnemonic and systematic point of view, they should also make reference to the meaning of the variables. The choice of variable names should not be left to an *ad hoc* decision by the individual programmers, but should be carefully planned by a co-ordinating body with a standardised approach. The same name should be used in all parts of an extensive software system. Constants that are used in several places in a program should be referred to by their name and not by their values; similarly with parameters that may change. The choice of labels should be made on a problem-oriented basis. It is also important to check that each label is actually used.

If it is necessary to abbreviate variables either to meet the constraints of a particular language, or to reduce the probability of error in writing the name, the following points may be of use (Jackson, 1967).

(1)   Every significant word within the name (up to a maximum of three words) should be abbreviated.
(2)   The leading letters should be chosen (since the leading part of a name is more important than the end).
(3)   Consonants are more important than vowels.
(4)   The abbreviation should not be larger than 15 letters.

Process Sections

The process sections of a program should, as far as possible, make use of tried and tested program sections, such as library programs. Related tasks, as already mentioned, are to be realised in function and procedure subprograms. Great attention should be paid to the initialisation of constants, variables and files, and particularly array indices, which should also be checked during program execution. Incorrect index values can often lead to non-specific error symptoms in a system. So that the user does not gain a false impression of accuracy, the calculation accuracy and the input and output formats should be in agreement. If any doubt exists as to the priority of execution of any of the arithmetic or logical expressions, then redundant parentheses should be used.

Control Structure

In accordance with the rules of structured programming (see section 6.1) only the control elements

IF   THEN   ELSE
DO   WHILE

should be used. This ensures that any given program section has only one start and one end point. Care is required even with use of these instructions. Thus for example the construction (Kernighan and Plauger, 1974a, p. 40)

IF ... THEN ... IF ... THEN ... ELSE ... ELSE

is considerably more difficult to analyse than

IF ... THEN ... ELSE ... IF ... THEN ... ELSE

In many cases complicated branching can be avoided by the use of simple logical operations on logical variables. Great care should be taken with equality comparisons in iterative loops. When using real arithmetic, unpredictable results may be obtained due to the inexactness of the representation of real numbers used for comparisons.

Normally the control flow of a program should proceed from top to bottom. If it is necessary to depart from this practice (for example, for efficiency reasons) or it is necessary to introduce the GOTO instruction, the program should be accordingly annotated.

The question of whether the GOTO should be avoided altogether, or whether it can be meaningfully used under certain circumstances has been the subject of numerous discussions. The various views have been discussed in an interesting article by Knuth (1974).

Input/Output

Many system errors can be directly traced back to a badly laid out input/output interface or a deficient check of input data. Input formats should be uniform and as free as possible. Input values or fields should be terminated by using special characters and not by relying on counting columns or cards. Input data, after a detailed application-dependent plausibility check, should be displayed to the user with an understandable identification. Similarly the results should be presented to the user with a clear text which explains the meaning of the numerical values. Similarly, error diagnostics should be comprehensible to the user.

With every software system a distinction can be made between the range of input determined by the application and the range determined by the representation of the data within the computer. Normally the application-determined range is a vanishingly small part of the range of values, which can be represented in the computer. From a reliability point of view, the range of input values should be kept as small as possible: first to reduce the probability of error on input, and second to increase the efficiency of the test procedures. Gilb (1973) suggests that the range of the input should be restricted to the most frequently expected input values. Additional identification must then be provided for unusual inputs before the system can deal with them, so that it does not reject them as random errors.

Testability

Every program should be written in such a way that it can be tested independently of the rest of the system. For this it is necessary that at important processing points intermediate results can be output, and data changed on request. These test aids should be retained in the final version of the program, to facilitate the implementation and testing of future changes. With real-time systems the test strategy should be defined at an early stage, since it can have a substantial effect on the system development.

Error Handling

All the possible errors that can occur in a program should be dealt with by the program itself, or passed back to the calling system. For a detailed discussion of error handling see chapters 9 and 10.

Commenting

It is not easy to comment a program meaningfully. In drawing up the comments it should be assumed from the beginning that the reader can understand the code used for programming as such. The comments should refer the code back to the formulation of the problem being solved. If it is necessary to explain the operation of a code by comments, it means that an obscure coding is being used and that it should be changed. A program may not only have too few comments, it may also have too many.

Each program module should start with a block of comments which should contain the following information

(1) program identification version and author
(2) date of production and the last modifications
(3) function of the module
(4) accuracy statement (especially in real arithmetic)
(5) input/output description
(6) assumptions regarding environment, side effects, etc.
(7) module limitations

(8)   error handling
(9)   sample calling sequence.

Furthermore, branch points within a program should be described with reference to the algorithm solution. Any program sections that probably will have to be changed as a result of program modifications should also be highlighted.

7 Verification of Software

At the beginning of every software development some concepts of what the system should do are formulated. The verification of the software package produced constitutes confirmation that these concepts are in fact fulfilled.

The reliability and correctness of software, or the existence of errors, may only be confirmed when computed test results from the program to be verified, or the program itself, are compared with acceptance criteria that have been prepared directly from the user's system requirements. The relationship between the specification, the acceptance criteria and the test results may be viewed as a 'test triangle', as shown in figure 7.1.

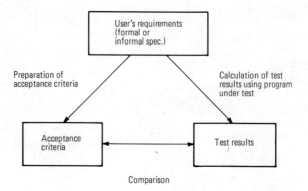

Figure 7.1   Test triangle

If the test results fail to meet the acceptance criteria then there is at least one error in the test triangle. Only when the assumption is made that the derivation of the test criteria is error free, and that the comparison of test results with the acceptance criteria has been carried out correctly, can the error be attributed to the program. No information regarding conditions outside the test triangle may be derived.

Table 7.1 shows how information regarding the correctness of a program may be obtained (Mills, 1973, p. 236).

TABLE 7.1

	Pragmatic	*Logical*
Program text	Visual checking of the source program	Analytical program verification
Execution	Testing with test data	Comprehensive testing of all input cases

7.1   TEST METHODS

Even with simple programs only a vanishingly small part of all theoretically possible input cases can be exercised during the test phase. This can be demonstrated by an example.

A program module has 3 inputs each of 16 bits and requires 100 μs of CPU for the computation. A complete test of all possible input cases (2^{48} is approximately 10^{14}) would require approximately 900 years of CPU time. In practice it is highly probable that the testing would be broken off after using less than 100 input cases. On the basis of the results of 100 test cases some statement will be made as to the behaviour for the complete 10^{14}. Since a purely statistical choice of test cases does not lead to conclusive information about the program, the importance of making the right choice in the selection of test cases becomes evident.

The above example also demonstrates that the program will encounter only a fraction of all possible inputs during its operational life. In deciding on the relevant test cases three approaches may be taken: to check the specified functions of the program, to select the test cases on the basis of the input distribution for the expected application, or to determine the test cases on the basis of the structure of the actual program. In the following sections these three test methods, the functional test, the acceptance test and the structural test, will be treated in more detail.

The Functional Test

During functional testing the specified functions should be tested individually and in combination. The software system is treated as a 'black box' by means of which expected results are calculated for given input values.

In the course of the functional testing it is useful to construct a test matrix (figure 7.2) which has on one axis the functions to be tested and on the other test cases. If a test case exercises a particular function then this is marked in the appropriate place. In this way the thoroughness of testing the individual functions and their combinations is shown in a manageable form.

The selection of relevant test cases on the basis of functional testing represents the most effective method of testing a program.

		Test case										
		1	2	3	4	5	6	7	8	9	10	11
Function	1	▨											
	2		▨										
	3	▨		▨									
	4		▨	▨	▨								
	5	▨				▨							
	6			▨			▨						
	7		▨					▨					
	8												
	9												
	10												

Figure 7.2   Test matrix for functional testing

The Acceptance Test

The acceptance test is developed from the point of view of the actual employ-
ment of the system by the user. The choice of test cases is made by the division
of the input space into application-related input regions. Important factors in
choosing these test cases are the problem-specific input cases (and their quantity)
in the various regions of the input space. The chief advantage of the acceptance
test lies in the almost complete covering of the development chain (see section
3.3) through a close co-operation with the user. The user, being the only one
who has authentic knowledge of the intended use of the software, should use
this knowledge in a comparison with the end results given by the software; he is
best able to pick test cases from the actual use of the system.

The main disadvantage with the acceptance test is the necessarily random
nature of the chosen test cases. Any statement as to the reliability of the software can be supported by statistical data only.

The Structural Test

This test method involves choosing a set of test cases based on the program
structure. The results of these tests in conjunction with a knowledge of the
program structure should build the basis of an inductive evidence for the correctness of software. The selection of the test cases can, for example, be made by
means of the following criteria.

(1) Every instruction in the program must be executed at least once.
(2) Every branch point should be tested, in each direction, at least once.
(3) All control paths must be tested.

The compilation of test data on the basis of the program structure is already a widespread procedure for the selection of the relevant test cases. Despite this, care should be taken since

(1) the testing of all possible paths is, even with a well-structured program, only possible in the smallest number of practical cases;
(2) the majority of programs are not complete, that is, not every instruction is explicitly checked to see if the operand is within the input space of the following operation. An incomplete program itself can, as a result of testing all of its control paths, be conditionally stated to be correct. The provision has to be made that all input errors will be recognised by any modules called (see section 9.2).

The structural test is a very effective method for the detection of error types IV and V (see section 3.1), since these errors have their cause in unintended side effects that should be found as a result of the execution of every instruction in the program.

Finally, it must be understood that even the conscientious use of any one or all of the test methods described is not sufficient to demonstrate that a practical program is error free.

7.2 TEST STRATEGIES

Program development (that is, the functional specification) proceeds in a top-down, from outside inwards fashion; the reverse (figure 7.3) is usually true in testing. Normally the individual modules are tested and then after integration with the complete system the system test is carried out. In conjunction with

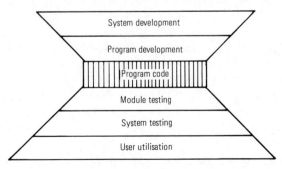

Figure 7.3 Sequence followed during system development and testing (Scherr, 1973)

structured programming it is suggested that the testing be carried out on a top-down basis also (IBM, 1971). Baker (1972) reports that the development of an extensive system for the *New York Times* avoided many of the problems that usually appear with system integration by adopting this procedure. The important control sections are almost incidentally tested during the system development. These sections are, however, especially important to the later reliability of the system.

The following sections deal with the individual test phases that must be gone through within the framework of the system development.

Desk Testing the System Design

The checking of the system design at the actual work-place of the programmers may be treated as the first phase in the testing. Such a detailed check of the system logic, by the processing of assumed input data, when consistently pursued can lead to the discovery of errors that otherwise would only first appear during system integration. The normally long time interval between the development of the system logic and the possibility of testing it on the computer, together with the often serious consequences of a logic error fully warrant this close scrutiny. On the other hand, a desk-top check of the program logic is not so important, since after its development it can be directly coded and tested out using the computer.

Module Testing

It must be borne in mind at the time of the system development that it will be necessary to test each module in isolation from the rest of the system. During the module testing, conditions should be similar to those that will be later encountered in the complete system. As few modifications as possible (for example, to make the module a stand-alone program) should be made, since these changes can introduce new errors. If the module under test calls other modules that are not yet ready, dummy modules which return values in the range expected by the calling module have to be used. To avoid the necessity of writing a complete test program for each module tested, it is usually sensible to develop a generalised module test program. Using this test program it is possible to generate test values and display the results.

Errors detected during module testing can usually be eliminated without difficulty. Errors detected at a later stage usually have more serious consequences. For these reasons module testing should be very thoroughly executed.

Integration Testing

The testing during the integration of a system has to be performed in several steps. After the introduction of a new module with new functions, it has to be established that the previously tested performance of the system has not been altered. This phase in the testing is known as a regression test. Only when this regression test has been successfully performed may the testing of the new functions begin. At the end of the integration test the reaction of the system to incorrect input data should be checked.

Performance Testing

Performance testing concerns itself with whether the actual system performance, such as CPU loading, response time, etc., corresponds with precalculated estimates. By comparing the actual performance with the planned performance it is often possible to discover disguised development errors (Scherr, 1973). The production of performance data is best achieved by using a hardware monitor, since a hardware monitor does not influence the software in any way. If on the other hand a software monitor is used, it is possible that the test results will be corrupted by the software monitor.

Test Aids

In complex systems testing requires between 30 per cent and 50 per cent of the total system effort. In order to reduce this effort a number of software packages designed to support the programmer during testing have been developed.

The first stage of testing requires the production of test data. As already mentioned this data should be selected on the basis of the program structure as well as from the expected input distribution. There exist a number of program packages for the support of structure testing which analyse the source text of the program under test to produce a set of test data that fulfils the given test criteria. A by-product of such an analysis is the thorough documentation of the construction of the program and the use of variables. At the same time a check is made to see if all program parts can be activated and which variables are decisive for the individual branch points in the program (Ramamoorthy and Ho, 1975). Other tests aids support the programmer with an inventory of test data for the acceptance test. A systematic or random choice of a number of records from an extensive supply of data may be made to build up an inventory of test data.

The programmer may also be supported by suitable software during the actual testing. A test supervisor program can produce and analyse statistics concerning the actual extent of a series of tests, and can, for example, display which program sections have been tested, which branch points have been exercised in all directions, and how much CPU time a subprogram requires. With the appearance of an error the relevant interrupt can be circumvented, the error displayed and the tests continued without loss of time. With a special module test program every environment that is likely to be encountered during the later use of the program may be simulated without too much effort. Especially with the testing of real-time programs, simulation programs are extremely important. Through the simulation of external conditions the real-time behaviour of a

system can be realistically tested without the problem of random, often un-
repeatable input situations. Many errors can thus be recognised and eliminated
before testing with real input data. In many situations with complex systems it
is an advantage to simulate the real world using an independent external
computer. Teleprocessing systems may be simulated when the output is short-
circuited to the input, and the system behaviour examined.

The checking of results obtained from extensive testing can often be very
laborious. The algorithms for producing comparison results should, where
possible, be different to those implemented in the program under test, so that
errors that appear in these algorithms may also be detected. Sadowski and
Lozier (1972) adopt the view that the only acceptable method of testing mathematical functions is with the aid of input-value pairs. Input-value pairs can be
verified independently of the algorithm under test. Rault (1973) suggests, on the
other hand the development of reference programs by means of which comparison
data can be produced. These reference programs can be conveniently written in a
high-level language without having to pay too much attention to efficiency. If
the test data and the comparison results are in a form that can be read by the
machine then the comparison may be made automatically.

The expected test results must be available before the start of the test.
Otherwise the programmer does not have any criteria at hand to judge the validity
of the results obtained during the test.

7.3   THE TEST PLAN

A detailed test plan can be extremely useful during system development. It is the
task of the test plan to define which functions and to what extent they will be
tested in each of the test phases. The test plan and the test strategy should be
simultaneously developed with the system specification before the system itself,
since these can have a profound effect on the system development (Brinch
Hansen, 1973b). It is sometimes necessary, even in the system design, to take
precautions so that the test philosophy can be adhered to.

The following should be included in a good test plan

(1)   a listing of all functions that are to be tested
(2)   a description of the test strategy that will be used
(3)   test criteria that must be fulfilled, such as percentage of branches and
        control paths, range of variables, etc.
(4)   error rate that must be achieved before the system can be classified as
        deliverable
(5)   performance requirements expected for the complete system and its
        components, such as CPU time, response time, etc.
(6)   a list of all errors that the system must be able to detect, with a state-
        ment as to how these errors are to be activated during testing and what
        consequence is related with each error

(7)   a statement of how the test results are to be documented as well as a classification scheme for errors
(8)   planned duration of the test phase
(9)   immediately before the test a list of all input values and expected results should be prepared.

7.4   ANALYTICAL PROGRAM PROVING

Whereas with testing an attempt is made to establish confidence in the reliability of a program by means of a point-by-point check of the input, analytical program proving concerns itself with the program itself as opposed to just the computational results using the program. The aim is to show by formal means that the program in itself is correct. In this case the correctness and not the reliability is investigated (see section 2.3). Although the correctness of a program may be demonstrated with varying degrees of stringency, including verbally, the advantage of formal methods lies in the exact definition of the rules and terminology and hence, in principle, the possible mechanisation of the proving.

A collation of the state of the art in formal program proving is to be found in London (1975).

What is understood by program correctness within the context of analytic program verification? According to Manna (1969) the question may be answered as follows.

Given: a program P, its input space D_x, its output space D_z, a predicate $\phi(x)$ defined over D_x (the 'input assertion' or precondition) and a predicate $\psi(x,z)$ defined over $D_x \times D_z$ (the 'output assertion' or post-condition);

then: a program P is correct with reference to the precondition $\phi(x)$ and the post-condition $\psi(x,z)$ when for all x of D_x the precondition $\phi(x)$ is true, the program $P(x)$ is defined and the post-condition $\psi(x,P(x))$ is true.

To ease the verification process, Floyd (1967) has suggested that in addition to the pre and post-conditions, additional conditions should be supplied, which must be fulfilled at important points within the program.

The introduction of these additional conditions means that the proving process can be reduced to a number of small steps and hence simplified. It then has to be shown that a given condition and the associated program section lead to the next condition. If this is not the case, then assuming that the intermediate condition has been correctly formulated, there is an error in the section of program investigated. The preparation of these intermediate conditions requires a high measure of intuitive ability, in addition to a fundamental understanding of the problem and a detailed analysis of the program.

After execution of an analytic program verification (mostly in a special high-level language), a program is assured of meeting its specification. In order to eliminate testing completely from programming, both the compiler and operating system must be formally verified. However, even then only a small part of the development chain cited in section 3.3 is covered. An error in the systems analysis or formulation of the functional specification will not be covered, just like an execution error.

The verbal specification of software systems outside the areas of logic or numerical mathematics already presents a considerable problem. However, considerably more difficult is the formal representation of these specifications and in particular the formulation of necessary and sufficient pre and post-conditions. If in addition there are time considerations to be taken into account, as for example with real-time systems, then there will be additional problems.

If it is possible to represent the intentions for a program and the acceptance test formally, it must in principle be possible to derive a program directly from its specification. This automatic program synthesis could be of great long-term interest.

The current situation with analytic software verification appears to indicate that in the near future it will not represent a viable alternative to program testing. Despite this, it is valuable to be familiar with this technique in order to gain a deeper insight into the programming task. Since the extent of the analytical proof can be taken as a measure of the complexity of a program, it is possible to uncover, by attempting the formal verification of certain paths, some unintended side effects that contribute to the complexity and hence the error susceptibility of a program.

8 *Manual Debugging*

Whereas during testing the task is to determine the presence of errors, that is the external observation of error symptoms, the task during debugging is to find the cause of these errors and to eliminate them.

8.1 MANUAL ERROR DIAGNOSIS

The elimination of each error entails several phases that are described in detail in the next section.

Reproducing Errors

As a first step in the debugging process an externally observed error must be reproduced. With permanent errors this is usually quite easy. The opposite is often true when transient hardware faults or timing conditions have to be taken into account. If the error cannot be reproduced at will, but only randomly, then the external conditions have to be varied systematically, so that the failure rate changes. The way in which the failure rate varies can often provide the first clue as to the type of error being sought. If variations in the environmental conditions (for example, temperature changes, artificially induced oscillations) have an effect on the failure rate, then in all probability the error is due to the hardware. If, however, the failure rate, under constant environmental conditions, alters with changes of the input distribution, there must be a design error in either the hardware or the software.

Error Diagnosis

If an external error is reproduceable, then the next step is to find the corresponding internal error. The location of the error is known as the actual diagnosis. In principle the diagnosis could follow the following procedure (Carter *et al.*, 1970, p. 313).

A particular input condition is set up and the resulting output observed. As a result of these observations further inputs are formulated and the procedure repeated until, making use of a knowledge of the program structure, the error has been isolated to such a small area of the program that it may be corrected or replaced. Carrying out such a procedure with the software can, however, have several problems associated with it, as follows.

(1)   The number of instructions between two observable interfaces is usually large. This means that the results of the individual test will localise the problem to large areas of the program.

(2)   It is very difficult to choose an input case which causes a precise over-lapping of the control paths of various computations to occur. Such precision is needed, however, if a combination of correct and incorrect results is to be used to localise an error to a small program area.

From the above considerations there are two main requirements that a system must possess if repeatable errors are to be diagnosed; these are observability and controllability (that is, the ability to inject chosen input conditions at various points in the program in order to select arbitrary control paths).

The diagnostic process can be considerably eased if the system is modular with well-defined interfaces. It will then often suffice just to inspect data at the individual interfaces in order to isolate the erroneous module. This demonstrates another advantage of data-oriented system design. The well-defined data structures, which contain the individual intermediate results, are relatively simple to inspect in order to determine their correctness. They represent a clear and unambiguous picture of the state of the interfaces at any given time. This measure of observability is not obtained with a program-oriented design. Since it has to be assumed that every program will contain errors, it is wise to make provision for debugging during the system design. Such built-in debugging aids, which have been designed for the specific system at hand, are often more effective

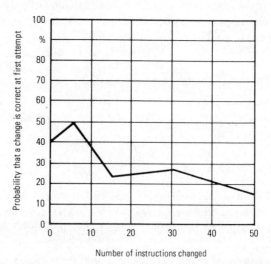

Figure 8.1   Probability of a change being correct at the first attempt as a function of the number of instructions being exchanged (Wolverton and Schick, 1972)

than general debugging tools (for example, general traces) which do not consider the characteristics of a given application.

Error Correction

Once the cause of an error has been ascertained, there may be several solutions to the problem of correcting it. Before any particular solution is adopted it must be exactly determined just which parts of the system will be affected by the proposed solution. Experience shows that very often the correction of one error introduces other errors. Figure 8.1 shows the probability of a successful correction as a function of the number of instructions that have to be changed in making the correction (Wolverton and Schick, 1972). Even if only one instruction is changed, the probability is less than 50 per cent that the first attempt will be correct.

If several choices exist, then the one that fits the existing structure best is the one to be preferred.

At the same time that an error is corrected the system documentation must be updated to the latest standard.

Checking Corrections

Naturally, after each error correction the system must be checked to determine whether the error actually has been eliminated and that no new errors have been introduced in the process. This test phase that must follow each correction can often entail much more effort than the actual correction.

8.2 DEBUGGING AIDS

There are several software products on the market which have been designed to support the programmer during debugging. This support consists of either the provision of special language instructions, or stand-alone software packages, which can be invoked during the running of the program and collect data which is later used for error diagnosis.

From the foregoing discussion the following requirements emerge as being essential in supporting the programmer during debugging.

(1) *Repeatability*   It must be possible for a once observed phenomenon to be repeated so that it can be examined in detail.
(2) *Observability*   During the uninterrupted running of the program it must be possible to examine the contents of the available data structures. Obviously this data must be presented in a form that the user can understand.
(3) *Controllability*   It must be possible to change any arbitrary data element without affecting the rest of the system. In particular it must also be possible to continue the program from any arbitrary instruction.

Although there exist many debugging aids — some of which are quite effective — a widespread method for diagnosing difficult errors has remained the core dump. The use of this method can be directly traced back to the over-optimism of the programmer. In the belief that the next program will be written without errors, the timely planning of debugging aids is considered unnecessary. Inevitably errors do occur, and hence, owing to the lack of any other means, recourse has to be made to the most primitive methods.

Interactive Debugging Systems

With an interactive debugging system the programmer is provided with a number of additional commands which may be used to observe and control the program during execution. To be successful such a system has to be a sensible compromise between the following two conflicting requirements.

The first requirement is that the dialogue must be simple and flexible. If the number of commands is small and the syntax compatible with the program language being used, then the additional learning task for the programmer is kept within reasonable bounds. The programmer must accept, however, that a certain amount of effort will be required before such a system can be put to practical use. In addition the system should be realised in a small area of the main store.

The second requirement is that the system should satisfy as many of the following requirements as possible

setting and deleting of break-points
checking and changing the value of a variable
error trapping
insertion of instructions
tracking of a variable value
changing the program flow
simulation of input and output
simulation of interrupts
reporting the statistics such as CPU time, running time, etc.

In implementing such a system the man—machine communication should be designed to suit the man and not the machine. An example of such a debugging system can be found in Grisham (1971).

The EXDAMS Debugging System

EXDAMS (Extendable Debugging and Monitoring System, Balzers, 1969) is an especially interesting example of a debugging system that meets the above-mentioned second group of requirements. The system provides the ability to collect data during the execution of a program that may be quietly analysed later. The system consists of two parts, one for data acquisition and the other for analysis. During execution of the program being debugged all important information concerning the program is recorded. The implementation of the data acquisition program does not give such extensive access to the program under test as an interactive system. The data recorded may subsequently be evaluated by the various analysis programs available in EXDAMS. It is possible to run the program both backwards and forwards, track the value of particular variables, determine the actual path taken during execution, and so on. If the user needs a special type of evaluation the facility exists for the incorporation of user-written software.

EXDAMS goes a long way towards meeting the twin requirements of repeatability and observability. However, no values can be changed during execution. Despite this, such a system can be of great assistance in debugging real-time systems, when a rapid sequence of events can be directly recorded and later analysed at leisure.

9 *Automatic Error Detection*

'Software should be designed to recognize silly situations and not be led astray by them.'

C. R. Spooner (1971) p.8

In the preceding chapters testing and debugging were treated as more or less manual processes. The following two chapters deal with these processes as being automatic. Computer systems that are able to recognise an error and take appropriate action are known in the literature as fault-tolerant systems. In recent years a new branch of computer science has been established to deal with the problems associated with fault-tolerant computing (Avizienis, 1978).

In principle there are two techniques for attaining a sufficiently high degree of reliability: either the use of extremely reliable components, or the use of a redundant structure where component faults can be detected and circumvented (see chapter 2).

Every manufacturing technology produces components with a characteristic reliability. If this characteristic reliability is insufficient for a particular application it can be increased, within certain limits, by taking extra precautions during production and by strict quality control. However, the cost of such increased reliability can grow rapidly. Fault-tolerant computing is adopted on the premise that it is more economical to build redundant systems than to strive for extreme reliability, even though it might be technically possible. The fault-tolerant technique has been used in particular in computer hardware (Toy, 1978). The technique can, however, also be used in software.[1]

The individual steps required for the development of automatic detection and·elimination of errors are similar, to a certain degree, to manual debugging. However, the automation of these steps requires formal implementation procedures and very close checking to ensure that there are no additional sources of error introduced into the system by the automatic mechanism.

---

1 cf. Walker, 1974, p. 263: 'Our philosophy with respect to recovery has been that for a large majority of applications, though certainly not all, it is much more cost effective to expect failures to occur and to recover rapidly from them than to aim for a total fault free system.'

9.1 ANALYSIS OF ERROR-DETECTION MECHANISMS

Every error detection presupposes that the result of a step in a process can be related to an acceptance criterion. If the result of the step meets the criterion then it is correct; otherwise it is false (with respect to the criterion). Automatic error detection is only possible when such criteria are available within the system. The system must therefore contain redundancy, meaning that there are more resources available than are absolutely necessary for the solution of the problem. In the following it will be assumed that these additional resources, which serve the purposes of error detection, can be collected together to form an error-detection module which may be separated from the actual processing. In practice the error detection can take widely differing forms, such as the mere testing of an overflow bit, or the execution of an extensive section of code which checks the results of a process step for plausibility. From the reliability standpoint the error-detection function is in series with the program (see figure 9.1); this means that an error in the error-detection module will have a direct influence on the reliability of the complete system.

The following analysis (Kopetz, 1975b) presupposes a simple system with one processing module and one error-detection module. The results obtained from this system may then be subdivided as follows.

(1) *Intended results*   those results that fulfil the intentions of the user and are therefore correct.
(2) *Actual results*   those results that are actually produced by the processing module.
(3) *Accepted results*   those results that are classified by the error-detection module as being acceptable.

Figure 9.2 shows these three sets of results in a two-dimensional diagram. Theoretically the three regions must completely overlap, but due to errors in the processing and error-detection modules they only partially overlap.

A distinction is now made between the following error types in the process and error-detection modules and their related probabilities.

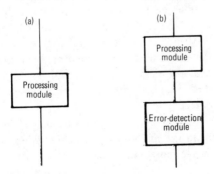

Figure 9.1 Systems (a) without, and (b) with error detection

Software Reliability

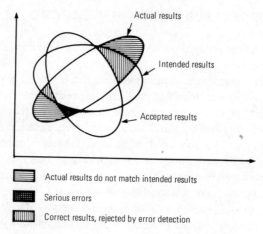

Figure 9.2   Relationship between actual, intended and accepted results

Processing Module

p_0 The probability that the module produces no results, that is a system break-down.
p_1 The probability that the module produces an unintended (hence incorrect) result.

Error-detection Module

e_0 The probability that the module produces no results, that is a system break-down.
e_1 The probability that the module rejects an intended (hence correct) result.
e_2 The probability that the module accepts an unintended (hence incorrect) result.

On the basis of the system structure (figure 9.1) and the error description, the relevant decision tree can be drawn and the probability of the error types introduced in section 3.1 derived (figures 9.3 and 9.4). Considering figure 9.5 it can immediately be seen that the reliability of a system that has error detection is inferior to a system without it. On the other hand the probability of type III errors, that is, that the incorrect results will not be detected, is strongly reduced (see also figure 3.1). It is only when error detection is introduced that type I errors can be detected and the input rejected.

The value of error detection can only be judged in the context of the particular application. In the majority of cases the reduction of the probability of incorrect results is far more important than the other consequences of the error detection.

In a real-time system that operates only once, the reliability requirements

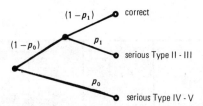

Figure 9.3   Decision tree for a system without error detection

may be such that mere error detection (without a consequent error correction) in itself can prove detrimental.

When a system must react to an external stimulus within an application-determined real-time interval, then an incorrect reaction may be less critical than no reaction at all. All real-life decisions do have an associated time parameter. Not deciding in time means not deciding at all.

Automatic error detection is a prerequisite for the reduction of serious errors and the introduction of errors of type I.

9.2   METHODS OF ERROR DETECTION

It is widely accepted that a substantial part of each extensive computer system must be concerned with the detection of errors in the hardware, software and input data. Primarily error detection prevents the occurrence of serious errors and transforms them into type I errors.

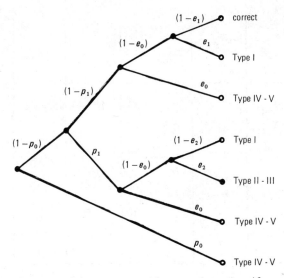

Figure 9.4   Decision tree for a system with error detection (for error types see section 3.1)

	System with no error detection	System with error detection	Ratio $\dfrac{\text{with}}{\text{without}}$
Probability of result being correct	$(1-p_0)(1-p_1)$	$(1-p_0)(1-p_1)$ $(1-e_0)(1-e_1)$	$(1-e_0)(1-e_1)$
Type I probability	—	$(1-p_0)(1-p_1)$ $(1-e_0)(e_1)\,+$ $+(1-p_0)(p_1)$ $(1-e_0)(1-e_2)$	—
Type II-III probability (data errors)	$(1-p_0)(p_1)$	$(1-p_0)(p_1)$ $(1-e_0)(e_2)$	$(1-e_0)(e_2)$
Type IV - V probability (system breakdown)	p_0	$(1-p_0)(e_0)+p_0$	$1+\dfrac{e_0}{p_0}-e_0$

Figure 9.5   The probability of various error types

Most computers contain hardware provisions for the detection of errors. Typical error indications are made on parity failure, incorrect instruction operation codes, or the erroneous transmission of data between the processor and its peripherals. Obviously provision must be made in the software for all these hardware error indications.

A further group of hardware indicators can be used to indicate software errors, for example, the use of an overflow indicator for arithmetic outside its permissible range, and the overwriting of protected data areas in the main core store. The program interrupts resulting from these error indications must lead to the software processes causing the error. In many systems the reliability is unnecessarily reduced because insufficient distinction is made between actual hardware errors and software errors discovered by hardware. With error detection a further distinction must be made between errors in the system nucleus and errors in the applications software. In this context the system nucleus means the central functions of the operating system such as error handling, resource management, and so on. Since the nucleus has more privileges than the applications software, an error in the nucleus is usually much more serious. On the other hand, the nucleus can be kept small and manageable by suitable structuring.

Some of the methods that can be used for error detection are now described. Of special interest are those that can be implemented in software form.

Protection Domains

With every program a number of characteristic domains in the data space and in the instruction space can be associated. Examples are the input domain for input variables, output range, data domains on backing storage, and the area where the program is stored in the main store. During the normal execution of a program all data elements must be within the domains assigned to the program. If this is not the case, there is an error in the system.

When several user programs are executed quasi-simultaneously in a machine, steps have to be taken to ensure that these programs and their associated data areas are protected from each other. For this purpose all objects with the same access characteristics are grouped together into protection domains.

The construction of these domains meets the requirements for the protection of information and for the provision of an easy and controlled exchanging of information. The problems associated with the security of access and the exchanging of data sets, especially in the construction of large data banks and data networks have grown rapidly in importance, and have not yet been completely solved. As far as software reliability is concerned, however, it is not the intended exchange of data that is of interest, but the unintended violation of domains by software errors.

The access to protected objects can be controlled by capabilities. A capability can be considered as a (hidden) parameter associated with a process and made available to the access procedure of a resource in order that this access procedure can check the legality of the access by this process (Brinch

Hansen, 1973a, p. 232). With the aid of capabilities one can construct selective access modes to particular objects, for example, partitioned areas of storage. If a domain is violated by an applications program, then a program in the protected operating system is invoked by hardware, which takes over error handling. Many machines offer selective access modes to partitioned areas of storage, such as read only, read and write, execution only. From the reliability point of view, the general use of these selective access modes should be strongly encouraged so that the consequences of a software error can be detected as close as possible to its source. The development of complex software systems should only be attempted when planned hardware offers the possibility of constructing such partitioned areas, since the execution of a completely correct program can be interrupted as a result of an addressing error by a parallel running program. It is, however, improbable that all parallel processes running will be error free. Thus for reliability it is advisable to provide each process with the bare minimum of access privileges, that is, only those absolutely necessary for the fulfilment of its task. This increases the probability of the early detection of an error. Furthermore, an error can then only affect a clearly defined and limited region.

Checking of Data Limits Imposed by the Program Structure

As already mentioned several times, the execution of a program module may be described as a process that transforms data from the input space into data in the output space. These input and output spaces have constraints imposed on them by the characteristics of the given application and the structure of the program. If the input and output of each computation are checked to see that they lie within these constraints, then certain errors may be detected. In the following the constraints which are determined by the program structure will be investigated (Kopetz, 1975a). The constraints imposed by the characteristics of the application are treated subsequently.

A software system with a hierarchical structure is assumed. The execution of a data transformation instruction, the internal structure of which is not relevant at this level of discussion, is taken as an elementary process. Every elementary process has a defined input and output space.

Partial Input Error Detection

The constraints imposed on a particular input space are partially imposed by the algorithm adopted in realising the program, and partially by the elementary processes called by the algorithm. Taking only the constraints imposed by the characteristics of the algorithm, these are termed the intrinsic constraints of the module or process. Examples of such intrinsic constraints are those that have to be imposed on the arguments of the series evaluation of a function due to the diminishing accuracy for large arguments.

Using the term intrinsic constraints, partial input error detection may be defined as follows (Kopetz, 1975a). A module possesses partial input error detection when all input values are checked against all intrinsic constraints imposed by the module.

Partial input error detection is not sufficient for the recognition of all possible input errors. Input errors related to elementary processes that must be called can always occur. If these elementary processes do not contain their own input error detection, then such errors can lead to serious errors such as incorrect results, or to a system breakdown.

Complete Input Error Detection

When an input case is checked not only against the intrinsic constraints imposed by the module, but also against all the constraints imposed on the input space by the elementary processes that are called by this module, then the module is said to possess complete input error detection. In this case all input errors associated with the elementary processes that are called will be detected.

The implementation of complete input error detection for a particular module requires an additional program section, which may be considerably more extensive than that needed for partial error detection. This can be demonstrated by a simple example as follows.

A program module contains the single instruction for division of one real number by another

$$C := A/B$$

In this module no additional code is required for partial input error detection since the division may be treated as an elementary process. For complete input error detection, however, the following conditions must be checked

$$|B| = 0$$
or $\qquad |A| \geqslant |B|.k \quad$ (underflow if false)
and $\qquad |A| \leqslant |B|.K \quad$ (overflow if false)

where k is the smallest real number that can be represented by the system and K is the largest real number that can be represented by the system.

It should also be noted that $|B|.k$ itself can lead to underflow if $|B| < 1$, and should be rearranged before programming. Similar considerations apply to the other conditions. From this simple example it is clear that the implementation of complete input error detection is by no means trivial.

When complete input error detection is implemented for every module in a hierarchically structured system, the additional program sections required lead to the following problems.

(1) *Reliability*   As previously mentioned, the possibility of errors in the error-detection process cannot be ignored. Since the error detection is in

series with the process, the introduction of a long section of code for complete input error detection will lead to a reduction of the reliability of the system (see section 9.1).

(2) *Performance*   The execution of the code required for complete input error detection requires additional processing time.

(3) *Maintainability*   If the constraints on the input space of an elementary process are modified for some reason, then all the modules that call these elementary processes must also be changed to preserve the complete error-detection mechanism.

(4) *Development effort*   A considerable increase in the development effort is required for the implementation of complete input error detection.

These problems are the main reasons why in many practical applications complete input error detection has not been introduced. From the standpoint of the complete system (as opposed to that of each of the modules) complete input error detection may also be implemented if every elementary process — whether in software or in hardware — contains a partial input error detection and the overall error handling is treated in the following manner. Each elementary process reports any error that may occur to the calling process. The calling process may then either take measures to circumvent the error or may itself report the error to the next higher calling process (see figure 9.6). When the highest level in the software hierarchy is reached, the (external) input case that caused the error can then be directly determined. The situation is then identical to that when the uppermost module has complete input error detection. This concept of systemised error handling has already been suggested by several authors (Hill, 1971; Parnas, 1972b). Unfortunately only few languages possess the necessary instructions for the implementation of this concept. It should be noted, however, that the complete detection of input errors only detects serious errors and transforms them into type I errors. No type of error detection can solve the problems associated with type I errors — the system is simply not in a position to process the intended input.

Plausibility Checking in the Software

The above described methods are independent of a particular application. In addition to these techniques it is possible and sensible to check intermediate and end results for plausibility as dictated by the particular application. These plausibility checks should be based not only on the program specification but also on the original statement of the problem (see figure 3.3), in which case system analysis errors may also be recognised. Plausibility checking should check on the one hand for the uniformity and completeness of data, and, on the other, on physical conformity with the invariants of the real world. Clearly these plausibility checks will be highly application-specific. They may be seen as an informal acceptance of the intermediate and end results obtained, just as the

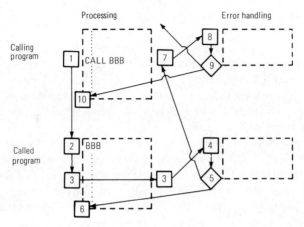

		Status
(1)	Call to subprogram	Processing
(2)	Automatic transfer of control to begin sub	Processing
(3)	Error occurs	Error
(4)	Automatic transfer of control to error handling	Error
(5)	End of error handling	Error
(6)	If error handling successful, continue normal processing	Processing
(7)	If error handling unsuccessful (or if error in error handling), return to calling program	Error
(8)	Automatic control transfer to error handling (analogous to (4))	Error
(9)	As (5)	Error
(10)	As (6)	Processing

Figure 9.6 Systematic error handling in a hierarchical software system

results of a calculation are roughly checked for their magnitude to see that they are approximately right.

In addition to those that are problem-related, program-specific plausibility checks should be used. These, for example, may take the form of chained data lists with forward and backward addressing, or the comparison of the actual hardware state with that expected.

Error-detecting Codes

The best known method for detecting hardware faults is by the use of error-detecting codes, such as, for example, parity checking. These methods are somewhat less important with software, although such codes as check sums are quite often used.

Timing Checks

A very effective way of detecting software errors is by the supervision of process execution times. This method applies to both system and user software.

To discover a failure of the system an external timing circuit which must be periodically triggered (say every second) is used. In the event of the circuit not being triggered over a period of more than one second the circuit reports an alarm indicating system failure.

The supervision of user software may be performed in an analogous fashion. The user software must report that it is running correctly by means of a short call of the system software within a given time interval. If this system call fails to take place then in all probability the user software contains an endless loop, which the system software can now recognise. An alternative approach is for the system software to allocate to each user process a maximum execution time, after which the process is automatically terminated.

Comparison of Independently Computed Results

If two sets of results are obtained from the same source input data using unrelated processes, and these results do not match each other, then it is certain that there is an error in at least one of the processes used. The term 'unrelated processes' may take the following forms

(1) the same process on the same hardware but at a different time (time redundancy, for the recognition of transient faults – Avizienis, 1972)
(2) the same process but on different hardware, at the same time (hardware redundancy, for the recognition of hardware faults – Wensley *et al.*, 1978)
(3) different processes, using different algorithms, running on the same hardware (software redundancy, for the detection of software errors)
(4) different processes, on different hardware, at a different time.

The methods of error detection by the comparison of independently computed results may also be realised purely by hardware and are thus completely transparent to the software.

Figure 9.7 contains a summary of the most important error-detection methods. It can be seen that data errors are much easier to discover than control errors. As was mentioned in chapter 4, this is one more reason for adopting a data-oriented system development.

9.3 ERROR-DETECTING INTERFACES

In the preceding section the error detection was treated as being completely separate from the actual processing. Every endeavour should be made to maintain

Error / Check	User software		Nucleus software	
	Data	Control	Data	Control
Protected area		X	X	
Data ranges	X		X	
Plausibility	X		X	
Error-detecting codes	X		X	
Timing		X		X
Dissimilar computation	X		X	

Figure 9.7 Summary of major error detection mechanisms

this separation during the system design, although this will not be possible for input errors imposed by the structure of the program. The necessity for this separation of the processing section from the error handling (the error-detection interface) is based on the following reasons.

(1) *Dissimilar Data Manipulation*   In the processing section data is changed, while in the error-detection section it is only checked, that is, only read. It is thus expedient to provide the error detection with limited access privileges in order to ensure that an accidental attempt at changing data during error detection will be immediately recognised.

(2) *Dissimilar Algorithms*   The different objectives of the processing and error-detection sections mean that different algorithms will usually be used. While in the processing section the main question is 'What is to be done?', the question in the error detection section is 'What is not allowed?'.

(3) *Testability*   The correct operation of the error-detection mechanism may be easier and more completely tested when it is realised in isolation from the processing section.

(4) *Maintainability*   In the event of a modification a distinction has to be made between the modification itself and its checking. When such a

distinction is made, errors introduced by the modification are more easily detected.

(5) *Restarting*   Since the integrity of a system is checked at the error-detection interface, this point may be used as a clear reference point for restarting the system. This is a prerequisite for any type of software redundancy.

If it is decided to collect all the error detection together into a single detection module, then the question arises as to where and how many of the error-detecting interfaces must be implemented in an extensive system. This question is partially answered by the objectives of the application, that is, which error types are most critical, and partially by the influence of the error detection on the reliability. In locating error—detection interfaces the following general points should be considered.

(1) *Input Data*   Since the probability of errors in the input data is relatively large, it must be checked for plausibility directly after input. It is therefore necessary to provide an error-detection interface after each input.

(2) *Error Propagation*   The positions of the error-detection interfaces determine how far errors may propagate without detection. It is thus necessary to analyse the consequences of error propagation before the position of the error-detection interface is finally decided upon.

(3) *Interchangeability of Components*   The size of the components (hardware components, software modules), which may be replaced in case of an error, obviously has an important role to play in deciding where to place the error-detection interface.

(4) *Restart Strategy*   As already stated a defined and correct system status is a prerequisite for restarting. The given application has requirements, such as the maximum permissible start-up time, which may partially determine where the error—detection interface must be placed.

(5) *Irrevocable Instructions*   With every real-time system certain events occur which lead to the execution of a section of the program which causes a permanent change in the environment; this is an irrevocable instruction — for (an extreme) example, the instructions for operating the ejection seat of an aircraft. Before such an irrevocable instruction is to be executed, the integrity of the system should be checked. In many cases it is advisable to defer the execution of the irrevocable instruction until the next error-detection interface has been reached. This helps to ensure that the actual processing is separated from the error detection.

10 *Automatic Error Correction*

'Rather, the point is that for the foreseeable future complex computing systems must, I believe, contain effective provisions for coping with software bugs as well as hardware failures, if such systems are to achieve really high reliability.'

B. Randell (1971) p. I.106

The automatic detection of errors gives considerable protection against serious errors . With batch processing systems this may be sufficient, since there is ample time available for the manual diagnosis of the error and its eventual elimination. In contrast to this, real-time systems will rarely allow for manual intervention since the time constraints may be very tight. Thus mere error detection is insufficient in such a situation. As was stated in the previous chapter automatic error detection also has a negative influence on reliability. Precautions must therefore be taken with real-time systems to ensure that the system becomes operational again in the shortest possible time – often within a fraction of a second. The new operating level, which is aimed for after an error has occurred, in general will not be able to support all the tasks expected of a fully functional system. This is, however, not critical with the majority of systems, since the requirements for a system are divided into primary functions, which must be fulfilled under all circumstances, and secondary functions, which may be abandoned in the event of the occurrence of an error (see chapter 3). Clearly a system that automatically corrects errors must contain considerably more redundancy than would be required for mere detection. The amount of this additional redundancy determines which error types may be circumvented. While the correction of transient errors requires data and time redundancy as well as software for restarting, correction of permanent errors requires additional hardware components and software modules. The automatic detection and correction of errors is essential in the construction of systems of extreme reliability. In computer applications where only short interruptions of continuous operation may be tolerated, an automatic restart of the system is required. The precautions that must be taken to provide automatic restart have a marked influence on the system design. It is not advisable to design the system first and then design the restart facility as an 'add-on'.

Although the recovery and restart facility is of great importance in almost any on-line application, there are still a lot of problems to be solved in this area; Verhofstad (1978) states: 'Another main conclusion is that there are still

enormous integrity and recovery problems to be solved for parallel processes
and distributed processing'. In the Electronic Switching System of Bell (the ESS)
35 per cent of the system outages is related to recovery deficiencies (Toy, 1978).

10.1 AUTOMATIC ERROR DIAGNOSIS

The formulation of the task of automatic error diagnosis is identical with the
manual diagnosis described in chapter 8. The diagnosis is, however, not performed
by man but by a digital system. A computer system can only recognise an error
if results that can be compared are produced by two independent subsystems.
According to Carter *et al.* (1970, p. 3.15), in order to enable self-diagnosis of the
overall system, the individual independent subsystems must execute the following
steps with reference to one another

(1)   the acceptance of a diagnostic procedure (see section 8.1)
(2)   the transmission of data to the system to be diagnosed
(3)   the acceptance of data from the system under diagnosis
(4)   the comparison of expected data derived from the diagnosis procedure
      with actual data from the system being diagnosed
(5)   the execution of branching dependent on the results of this comparison
(6)   the transmission of the results of the diagnosis.

A complete self-diagnosis capability requires a special structure in both the
hardware and the software.

In many cases a partial self-diagnosis capability will be sufficient. Partial
self-diagnosis assumes a diagnostic subsystem whose function must be postulated,
since an error in such a system can no longer be diagnosed automatically. It is
thus expedient to keep the extent of the diagnostic subsystem as small as possible,
that is, to use as few as possible of the functions of the hardware and programs
to start the diagnosis. This objective may be attained by using an iterative
procedure in the building of the diagnostic system. One starts with a minimal
diagnostic capability, which relies on the function of a few instructions, requires
little core store, and is resident in a read-only store. First the availability of all
resources that are required for the full diagnostic system is checked. If these
resources are completely operable, then the next phase towards a fully automated system recovery may be started. The minimal diagnosis system forms
part of the overall system nucleus. The extent to which the functions of the
system nucleus should be protected by additional redundancy depends on the
reliability demanded and on the estimated failure rate.

Avoiding Error Propagation

The first reaction to the detection of an error must be the prevention of its
propagation. For this purpose it is necessary to classify the error symptoms
as critical or non-critical.

Errors that may influence the operation of the system nucleus are classified as critical. Errors that belong to this group are those that can occur in the innermost layers of the operating system, or in hardware components that are required for the functioning of these innermost layers. In the event of such an error occurring, the entire system, including all application programs, must be forced into a controlled shut-down so that an extensive diagnosis may be performed. In all other cases — from experience by far the greater number — only selected application processes need to be suspended.

Actual Error Diagnosis

As already mentioned, error diagnosis involves tracing an externally observed error to the internal error causing it. An error can be said to have been successfully diagnosed when it has been traced to the smallest component that may be replaced. Before a diagnostic procedure can be developed, the size of the smallest component that may be replaced must be defined.

It is also possible that an error is undiagnosable, if the information available at the time of error detection is insufficient for the diagnosis, and there is no possibility of generating this information. There seems to be a relationship between the information available at the time of error detection and the effort required to diagnose the error.

An observable error in a computer system may be the result of a hardware fault, a software error, incorrect input data or incorrect operator action. Many of the immediate error causes may be directly inferred from the error signal, such as hardware parity, division by zero, protected memory violation, and so on. The underlying cause of an error may be ascertained from a further tracing of the error signal, and a suitable arrangement of the error-detection interfaces. Clearly the error need only be traced up to a component or module which may be replaced by redundancy.

Thus extensive hardware error detection, such as store parity, is required for the development of reliable systems, so that in the majority of cases hardware faults may be diagnosed directly by an error-detection mechanism.

If an error symptom cannot be attributed to a hardware fault (as signalled by the hardware) then it must be assumed that an input error or software error is present. If there is an application-dependent input error detection in the system, which classified the input case as correct, then it must follow that a software error is present.

After an error has been detected, a number of options remain open

(1) rejection of the input case which caused the error
(2) correction of the error symptoms and continuation of processing
(3) reconfiguration and restart.

Before any one of these alternatives is chosen, an error documentation must take place.

Error Documentation

Although the majority of errors may be diagnosed in the manner described, it is inevitable that the automatic error diagnosis will encounter situations where it will not meet with the desired success. So that such cases can be later diagnosed manually, it is essential that after the occurrence of error indication the most important symptoms of the error are recorded in a special error file. The following information should be recorded in such a file: the date and exact time when the error was detected, active hardware components, instruction and operand addresses, the type of error indicated, and the important system state variables.

Furthermore, each individual hardware subsystem should have an error counter. When it is suspected that an observed error can be traced back to a transient fault of a hardware subsystem, then the error counter for each active hardware subsystem should be incremented. In this way hardware that has a tendency to transient faults can be detected.

The recording of errors is also necessary in determining which errors have been circumvented by redundancy. In this respect the following observation by Scherr (1973) regarding the IBM TSO operating system is of interest: 'In any complex system designed to recover from its own or its users' errors, there is enough redundancy so that many errors successfully pass through the functional test cases and can be detected only because the performance of the system is not what it was expected to be.'

10.2 RECONFIGURATION

Reconfiguration is only necessary with the occurrence of a permanent error. If the observed error is of a transient nature, that is, only of short duration, then the error-detection mechanism can initiate a restart.

Since transient errors are more frequent than permanent errors in the hardware, once an error has been detected a second attempt at executing the relevant command should be made; this is the so-called retry. It is only after a fruitless retry that the system must be reconfigured. In many computer systems the retry is already implemented in the hardware in such a way as to be completely transparent to the software.

The retry process requires the provision of buffer registers where the operand may be retained until the original operation is successful. With microprogrammable computers the retry can be executed on the microprogram level, which can have considerable time advantages. The same applies also to errors that occur in the transmission of data to a peripheral. The I/O operation should be repeated until the existence of a permanent error can be established.

It can also appear in the software that, due to unintentional interference, an error will occur once only and is apparently not repeatable. However, by its very nature a software error can only be permanent. The phenomenon observed in practice, whereby a process runs correctly but in switching over to a second parallel running process an apparently random error appears, indicates an unintentional coupling of the two processes. This coupling is certainly reproducible if the input to each process is seen as the input data in the time domain. Software errors may thus only be circumvented when either the particular input is rejected or modified (for example, the abandonment of parallel processing), or redundant programs, which have a different development history, are activated.

Hardware Reconfiguration

At the conception of a redundant system it has to be decided at what level the redundancy is to be implemented — whether at system level (that is, a duplex system), subsystem level, or at component level.

Current hardware development suggests that in the future the greatest advantage will be derived from the use of redundancy of clearly delineated subsystems. This type of redundancy increases in efficiency in proportion to the number of identical, and hence interchangeable, subsystems used. Using microprocessors a great number of diverse problems can be solved using physically identical hardware within the overall system. The existence of such identical hardware components provides a convenient prerequisite for reconfiguration after an error. Similarly, a system that employs virtual addressing may circumvent an error in a block of the main store with relative ease (Neumann *et al.*, 1973, p. 58). Reconfiguration of failed peripherals may also be achieved without difficulty provided that it has been foreseen in the system design.

A few interesting projects (SIFT, Wensley *et al.*, 1978) have concerned themselves with the development of fault-tolerant systems by using a number of identical small computers. In such systems it is possible to achieve a pronounced increase in reliability with relatively little redundancy. A corresponding increase in the reliability of a large centralised system using only a few identical subsystems can only be achieved with a considerably increased effort.

The construction of distributed data networks from a large number of small computers is, from a reliability point of view, more appropriate than the control of a data network from a large central computer. Should one of the nodes drop out then an automatic reconfiguration of the network will ensure that only nodes directly connected to the faulty node or transmission line will be affected.

Software Reconfiguration

To date, experience with complex software systems has indicated that it is not possible to eliminate all design faults in such systems. Even after the very thorough tests of the Apollo software, errors appeared in the actual use of the system (Wolverton and Schick, 1972). Due to the substantial improvement in computer hardware, software errors determine to an increasing degree the overall system reliability. In addition to the introduction of newer methods for software development, some thought has been given to circumventing software errors by means of software redundancy (Randell, 1975; Kopetz, 1974). This may be achieved by means of standby redundancy. As soon as the system detects an error, special software sections are activated to perform the error handling. This type of error-handling mechanism is similar to the handling of hardware errors in the innermost layer of the operating system. Since it must be assumed that in the course of time ageing faults will appear in the hardware, it almost goes without saying that a careful system development will take such faults into account. If it is accepted that software errors cannot be entirely eliminated – it follows that redundant program sections should be provided for the handling of software errors. The planning of explicit error handling on every level of the software should be treated as a matter of routine and not as an exception. In addition to the normal processing sections, error detection and alternate processing sections are required. If an error is detected by a processing or error-detection module, then the system goes into an error status and executes the various levels of the error-handling processes until the error has been eliminated, the particular input case has been rejected (see also section 9.6), or at least the error symptoms have been corrected.

Whether the results from the processing module are rechecked by the error-detection module depends on the objectives of the entire system. The case shown in figure 10.1a gives a higher reliability since it covers repeated errors in the error-detection module, whereas an error in the standby module will go undetected. In the case of the configuration of figure 10.1b, errors in the standby will also be detected; however, the case can arise where a correct result will be rejected twice due to an error in the error-detection module.

It is not sufficient to make the standby module a direct copy of the

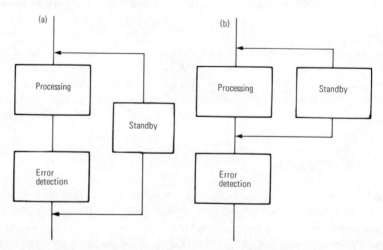

Figure 10.1 Different arrangements of the processing, error-detection and standby modules. Model (a) as Kopetz, 1974, (b) according to Randell, 1975

processing module, since in contrast to the hardware, only design errors exist in the software. The two processing modules must be realised in dissimilar ways, using different algorithms. The primary and secondary functions that have already been mentioned can form the basis for the implementation of software redundancy, since the standby module need only guarantee the primary functions. The difference of the requirements for the normal processing module and the standby module means that their development may be separated from each other, thus reducing the probability that the same design error is introduced in both modules. In order to ensure that the two design processes are different, it is advisable to allocate the tasks to two separate design teams.

10.3 RESTART

While with simple batch processing systems it is relatively easy to start completely afresh after an error has interrupted processing, the same cannot be said of extensive on-line and real-time systems. For these, such a 'cold start' has the following difficulties associated with it.

(1)   A number of parallel processes must be restarted from the beginning; the time lost may be great.
(2)   The computing system must be resynchronised with its environment.
(3)   The real-time constraints that exist will not allow the required actions to be performed in time.

Consequently, after the detection of an error, it is necessary to allow all the processes not directly affected by the error to run undisturbed. The difficulty of restarting grows with the complexity and number of system components involved; it is thus advisable to limit the processes to be restarted to the smallest number possible.

Restart Extent

If a data processing system is treated as a hierarchically structured system, then a restart should be possible on almost any level. A restart on any given level must not affect any higher level. If, for example, an I/O error disappears as a result of a retry, then higher processes should not be aware that the error has occurred.

In figure 10.2 four levels of restart are shown. In a strongly structured system, of course, many more levels may exist.

On the lowest level, the level where the error has least affect on the system, the erroneous function is re-executed (cf. functional restarting, Higgins, 1968), for example, repeated I/O operations. Since this level of restarting remains transparent to the remainder of the software, it must be considered to be one of the most elegant methods of overcoming errors.

At the next level the process affected by the error is suspended and if possible restarted. The rest of the system remains unaffected by the error.

	Functional restart	Process restart	Warm start	Cold start
Extent	local	local/global	global	global
Consequences for the user	none	moderate	moderate /large	large
Loss of computing time as result of restart	negligible	slight	moderate /large	very large
Assurance of data integrity	no problem	complex	complex	simple to complex
Special hardware required	large	slight	slight	simple
Software required	slight	large	large	slight to large
Time required for system reinstatement	slight	moderate	moderate	large

Figure 10.2   Various stages of restarting

Clearly, there already now exists a requirement for extensive measures to be taken to ensure the integrity of data.

If process restarting does not meet with the required success, the next level of restarting, known as the warm start, has to be tried. This involves suspending all processes, even those that have not been affected by the error.

As a final measure the so-called cold start is used, where the entire system is re-initialised. This usually means that a great loss of computer time is unavoidable. In addition a major effort may be required to establish a defined state of the data for the re-initialisation of a system with a large data base.

Establishing a Defined Data State

Establishing a defined state of the data after the occurrence of an error can be treated as having two aspects: the physical security of the data so that data can be recovered after a fault affecting a storage medium; and the logical consistency of the data, ensuring that all incomplete transactions at the time of error must either be completed or completely deleted from the system. The solution to these problems is very difficult; at present there appears to be no satisfactory general solution. Every known method, to date, presupposes that considerable precautions have been taken during the system design to enable the restoration of a defined data state after an error.

One method of securing data is periodically to store the state vector during normal operation in an independent store (at the so-called 'rollback-point'). If an error occurs the system is reset to the last rollback-point and the processing repeated from there. Since the storage of the data required to establish the rollback-point requires time that would otherwise be available for processing, and the restart time depends on the elapsed (real) time since the last rollback-point, the optimum frequency of rollback recording can only be established for each individual application in the light of the maximum tolerable restart time. Chandy *et al.* (1975) have developed a model which allows for the optimisation of the spacing between rollback-points.

If the state vector is of limited extent, the rollback method may be completely adequate to establish the defined data state. With larger data files the periodic storing of the state vector may cause longer interruptions of the normal processing than the particular application will allow. The problem may be further complicated when the storage of data is overlapped with normal processing so that it is very difficult to establish a meaningful reference point. In such a case it is necessary continuously to record the changing data together with both the new and old contents of the data records that have been changed (Verhofstad, 1978). Randell (1975) suggests a largely automatic (that is, embedded in the hardware) method of establishing a defined data state after the detection of an error. This method entails using a special hardware device called a 'recursive cache' which stores all the original data that is altered during a computation in a push-down store. This data is then retrieved to re-initiate a computation in the event of an error. The properties of a push-down store enable its use also in the restart at various hierarchical levels.

The Actual Restart

In order to find a relevant data state from the data state that is available at the time of restarting the system, all 'important inputs' that have occurred since the compilation of the available data state must be reprocessed, analysed and eventually repeated. The term 'important inputs' in this context means any input that leads to the alteration of a file in the system.

During the actual restart particular attention should be paid to the following points.

(1)   *Irrevocable Instructions* (see section 9.3)   If any irrevocable instruction has been executed in the interval between the establishment of the last rollback-point and the appearance of the error, then this has to be taken into account during the restart. Clearly a completely defined data state must also contain all relevant information regarding irrevocable instructions.

(2)   *Changes in the Environment*   It is possible that changes in the environment may take place during the restart. New data may be continuously offered up for processing. This data must be stored temporarily so that it can be dealt with later by the system when it is running again.

(3)   *Possibility of an Error* occurring during the restart cannot be completely discounted. Experience shows that the software for the detection and elimination of errors has often been very badly tested and possesses a poorer reliability than the rest of the system. In the ESS system, 35 per cent of the overall system outage is related to recovery deficiencies (Toy, 1978).

11 *Software Maintenance*

The development of a system can be said to be complete as soon as it is taken over by the user after the acceptance test. Any work that must be performed on the system after acceptance to support a particular state of the software is known as software maintenance.

11.1 THE REASONS FOR SOFTWARE MAINTENANCE

The need for software maintenance arises for several reasons.

(1) *The Correction of Errors that were Not Discovered during Testing*   The error rate of a software system is dependent on its error function (see section 2.3) and on the expected input distribution. Operational conditions can change the input distribution substantially, which may lead to a discrete jump in the error rate. Under software maintenance these errors must be corrected and the error rate returned to an acceptable level.

(2) *Change of System Requirements*   The definition of functional requirements of every successful system will change during the operational life of the system. In many cases the user himself is not in a position exactly to define the tasks that the system must perform. Not until practical experience with the new system has been gained does it become known what additional functions are desirable or even essential.

     A further need for change may result from the dynamics associated with the organisation which implements the computer application. Every company experiences such internal dynamics: improvements in technology, adaptation of the organisation to new conditions, new marketing requirements, and the inauguration of a successful software system, all offer the user new opportunities for rationalisation which were not thought of at its inception. The net result will be a requirement to change the system.

(3) *Changes in the Hardware Configuration*   Advances in computer hardware technology produce equipment which may offer a more cost-effective solution to a particular application. If full advantage is to be taken of these advances then both hardware and software have to be updated periodically. A further reason for changing the hardware configuration may be the extension of the application, resulting in the installed capacity being insufficient, and the need for larger equipment.

(4)   *Improved Performance*   Often it is only after operational data becomes available through systematic measurements with hardware and software monitors that the true relationship between the system components can be determined. By systematic changes and improvements it may then be possible to eradicate bottlenecks and substantially improve the system throughout.

The above reasons for change are largely outside the influence of the system developer. Dijkstra (1972a) states that every extensive and successful program will be issued in many versions during its lifetime, and that each new program only represents the starting point for a whole family of programs that will be used in practice. The expenditure on software maintenance can be considerable. A survey of 905 British computer users (Hoskyns, 1973) reveals that an average of 40 per cent of the total software effort was spent on mainten- ance (figure 11.1). In an established EDP department, that is, one that already possesses an extensive program library, software maintenance can take up to 80–90 per cent of the software support. In such departments program main- tenance ties up substantially more capacity than software development.

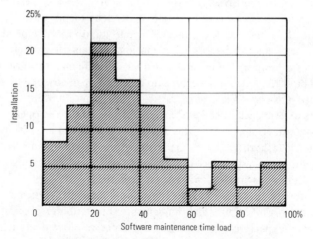

Figure 11.1   Average effort required for software maintenance from a study of 905 English computer users (Hoskyns, 1973)

Owing to the fact that during the lifetime of a successful software product more effort often has to be put into maintenance than into any other phase of the development, maintenance costs can be a most important factor in the soft- ware life cycle (Sloughter, 1974). The ease with which a system can adapt to new conditions is therefore decisive for its life expectancy. One of the most important tasks of software technology is to analyse and solve the problems of software maintenance.

11.2 FACTORS WHICH INFLUENCE THE MAINTAINABILITY OF SOFT-WARE

Every time maintenance is performed, for whatever reasons, the modification of a fully tested system is required, the direct consequences of which are difficult to foresee.[1]

It is only during the development of the system that the maintainability can be influenced to any degree. The earlier a decision is made during development, the more difficult it is to change at a later date (Parnas, 1971), since it is these decisions that dictate the course of the later design. As a result the first task during development is to determine the areas that are least likely to change. A prerequisite for this is that already during the system analysis some effort is spent in assessing the probability of later modifications in certain areas.

A look at some of the more specific factors, which do have an influence on the maintainability of a software system, gives the following list

availability of qualified software staff
understandable system structure
ease of system handling
use of standardised programming languages
use of standardised operating systems
standardised structure of documentation
availability of documentation which is designed for maintenance purposes
availability of test data sets
built-in debugging facilities
expandability of the system
availability of a computer system which can be used for software development.

It is possible to group these factors under the headings of understandability, standardisation, documentation, testability and expandability.

Understandability

Understandability has two aspects, the availability of software staff who are familiar with the system and accessible for maintenance work, and the intelligibility of the system *per se*. Since intelligibility is decidedly the most important criterion by which the structure of a system is judged (see chapter 4 on software structure), the objectives for a clear structure and easy maintainability are almost identical.

---

1 See for example, Spier, 1975: 'By and large, the re-opening of an existing software package, for whatever reasons, is considered bad medicine indeed, because of the high likelihood that any modifications might provoke undesirable side effects. Not a great many systems can tolerate the modification of existing critical modules, in so far as the radical replacement of critical modules by totally new versions thereof is concerned, few indeed are the systems, which gracefully can survive such a transplant'.

Standardisation

In many cases it will not be the original software developer but some other person who has to maintain the system. In such a case it can be decisive for the maintainability of the system that standard approaches and tools have been used during the original system development. It might even be wise to restrict oneself to a defined subset of a programming language and system facilities which will be supported by some future system of the same or some other vendor.

The early standardisation of FORTRAN and COBOL is one of the reasons for their wide acceptance in the industrial community.

Documentation

The documentation for maintenance purposes will be different from the documentation developed during system design. The documentation must be designed from the point of view of changes and modification. What effect will the modification of a certain section of a system have on the rest of the system? It is always good practice to check a given design from the point of view of possible modifications and to document the result of such a check for maintenance activities, which might be required later on. A standard for the structure of the documentation can considerably reduce the time required to find the way through the documents of an unfamiliar system.

Testability

Since every modification makes a new system out of a given system a complete retest of the system is necessary. All that has been said about testing in chapter 7 has a direct relevance to maintainability.

Expandability

A software system is expandable when it is possible to introduce a desired change in the logically relevant location. The introduction of these altered or additional codes should not increase the connectivity in either the data or instruction spaces. It is advisable to make the store allocation as flexible as possible and make provision for eventual alterations during the system design.

11.3 SOFTWARE MAINTENANCE AND COMPLEXITY

In practice the error rate of a system that has experienced numerous modifications initially decreases, reaches a minimum and then increases again (Ogdin, 1972). This property of the error rate can be explained by the influence of maintenance on reliability. Initially, directly after the commissioning of the system, previously undetected errors are corrected. Later on, the changes introduced during maintenance disturb the original system structure as conceived and there is an attendant increase in connectivity between the system components. This is equivalent to an increase in complexity and results in a reduction in reliability. Belady and Lehman (1971) in 'Programming Systems Dynamics or the Metadynamics of Systems in Maintenance and Growth' have attempted to determine a maintenance strategy through a model of the relationship between maintenance and system structure.

Starting with data on the maintenance effort required for a large software project, theoretical relationships for the increase in complexity due to maintenance changes were developed. Each alteration leads to a new release, the structure of which no longer corresponds exactly with the original structure and must be treated as a special case in future. This new release has similar dynamics to the original system. Errors appear that must be corrected, and changes must be made. As a result of these modifications it is found that the increase in maintenance has an exponential growth. Taking into account the learning effect and the familiarity of the programmer with the system, Belady and Lehman (1972, p. 505) develop the following expression

$$W = A + K \exp (C - D) \tag{11.1}$$

where W = total effort for the generation of a new version
A = productive effort
C = measure of complexity, resulting from the absence of structure
D = familiarity factor
K = constant

The first term is a measure of productive maintenance effort; the second is a measure of unproductive yet unavoidable effort caused by previous alterations, such as for example, additional coupling, side effects, and so on.

The difference in the exponential term represents a trade-off between complexity and familiarity. The complexity factor C is a property of the system since it depends on the coupling. Familiarity is largely programmer-subjective. A programmer new to the system will clearly require more effort to achieve a certain degree of familiarity, which in turn depends on the availability and quality of documentation.

At the beginning of the maintenance phase familiarity with the system often grows more rapidly than the complexity; the unproductive effort thus declines. In the long term the growing complexity outweighs the advantages of familiarity. As may often be observed in practice, the productive part of the maintenance steadily reduces, alterations become increasingly difficult to introduce and delivery dates for changes become longer. These phenomena indicate the approaching end of the system life.

When a high degree of complexity C, is balanced by a high degree of familiarity D in equation 11.1, then a system has associated with it a high maintenance risk. If, for whatever reason, a maintenance group that is thoroughly conversant with a system is suddenly lost, then the full consequences of the complexity

have to be borne. From this point onwards hardly any maintenance can be performed — a thorough reconception is required. This is a frequent occurrence with
systems that have been quickly developed to a relatively high standard by a small
highly skilled group. The break-up of the group then often means the end of such a
system, since an outsider will rarely be able to overcome the complexity which is
often accompanied by a poor documentation.

From a reliability point of view the slowest possible growth of the complexity should be striven for. This means that any proposed change must be carefully planned and conformity with the existing structure maintained. Lindhorst
(1973) suggests that maintenance should not be carried out on an *ad hoc* basis
but in order to meet defined delivery dates. All proposed maintenance alterations
can thus be simultaneously analysed and implemented. Such a planned maintenance strategy — provided it can be organised properly — has a very positive
effect on the reliability and life expectancy of a system.

As already mentioned, the quality of the functional specification is of
great importance to the later commissioning and maintenance of the system. If a
large number of unanticipated situations occur during the commissioning of an
extensive software system, numerous modifications have to be made before the
system is handed over to the user. This implies that already in the commissioning
phase a part, often a large part, of the life expectancy of the system has been
consumed.

12 *The Management of Reliable Software*

'Hence the man month as a unit for measuring the size of a job is a dangerous and deceptive myth.'

F.P. Brooks (1974) p. 46

The development of reliable software is not merely a technical problem but also a management problem. In the present context management may be understood to mean the attainment of all predefined objectives in a set time with the available resources. The usual management methods are planning, organisation and control. One reason for the frequent failure of software management is the difficulty of adapting these techniques to software development.

This final chapter dealing with some of the aspects of software management is included since the view is held that only after a thorough understanding of the technical processes of software development is gained can a software project be effectively supervised.

12.1 THE DIFFICULTIES OF SOFTWARE MANAGEMENT

The following sections analyse the difficulties that are characteristic of software management as a starting point for their solution.

Product Visibility

If a comparison is made between the production of software and a more conventional article, then the first great difference between the products appears. The software end-product consists solely of a set of carefully documented instructions for the computer; there is no tangible software product. The supervision effort required in determining development progress can be comparable with the development effort (Ellingson, 1973). A subjective estimate thus has to be made on the advice of the software developer. Figure 12.1 shows a typical example, which may often be observed in practice, of how such an estimate corresponds to the actual situation. Such a gross distortion results principally from the psychological situation of the programmer and from the great variation in the difficulty of the various phases encountered during development.

Metzelaar (1971) has investigated the productivity (measured as object code) during development as a function of the complexity for various software

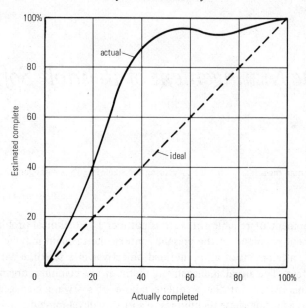

Figure 12.1 Estimated versus actually computed software during a project (Boehm, 1974a, p. 2.2)

projects, and has determined that it fluctuates strongly between simple and difficult (figure 12.2). Since there are also fluctuations in complexity within the same project, it can often happen that the time required for the last 20 per cent of the task (which is certainly the most difficult part) is greater then that required for the first 80 per cent. Thus when a project is already 80 per cent implemented it may well be that less than half of the actual work has been completed.

Lack of Physical Constraints

Software as a product of the intellect is not bounded by the constraints of hardware technology. The development of conventional products is constrained by the laws of nature between relatively narrow limits (for example, the properties of materials), whereas the limits for software are set by complexity and the ability of the human intellect to cope with it. The constraints due to complexity are very difficult to explain and quantify for people who are not experienced in the field of software development. It is therefore necessary that each computer specialist be highly self-critical and be aware of his own limitations in any given situation.

The lack of physical constraints is also responsible for the often incorrect view that software is easy to change, does not require a long development time and can easily be made to fulfil new conditions In contrast to this view, practical experience has prompted the following statement to be made by Boehm (1974a,

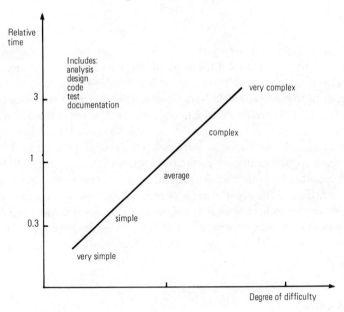

Figure 12.2 Relative time required per instruction as a function of degree of difficulty (Wolverton, 1974)

p. 8.5): 'It is often easier and cheaper to make a change to the hardware than the software'.

A further effect of the refusal to recognise the limitations imposed by complexity leads in many cases to the very superficial precautions taken for the handling of software errors.

Technological Changes

The rapid advances in both hardware and software make the software planning task particularly difficult. By the time that an extensive software project has been successfully concluded, economic grounds alone preclude a similar project on the same hardware and software basis. The result is that experience gained on an early project can only be adapted to a new project with difficulty.

Uniqueness

The development of a software system is a unique process as opposed to routine mass production. As with the construction of every unique product it is difficult to establish the usual norms such as progress and productivity. This may also be the reason for the often extremely poor documentation and maintainability of software, since it is easy to underestimate the effort required for documentation by adopting the attitude that it is only for a single product anyway.

Personnel

The success or failure of a project depends to a large extent on the personnel involved, due to the unusual difficulties of planning and control already described. The variation of ability between individuals is, however, particularly pronounced in the software field, variations of 1:10 and more not being unusual (Sackman, 1970). Software development requires creative personnel who can work with accuracy. However, creativity is often connected with characteristics which can lead to problems in personal relationships (Weinberg, 1971). A further point is the training of computer personnel. Any formal EDP training must be supported by project work that is at least as intensive in order to gain its full benefits. Due to the rapid expansion in the field, however, it often happens that the successful project worker is assigned to management tasks and directly after gaining the relevant experience is lost to software development. It is left to the reader to imagine the consequences arising from these difficulties for planning and control.

12.2 PLANNING

The basic prerequisite for good management is the existence of a realistic plan by which the project can progress.

A substantial part of all planning is the subdivision of the total effort required into a number of visible and supervisable parts. This is particularly important with software, in order to increase the poor tangibility of the product. As far as it is technically possible, an extensive software project should be subdivided in such a way that a small team can complete small independent sections of the work with checkable and useful results in a reasonable time interval. As a basis for reference for the size, take a team of between 3 and 6 people working for a period of 6 to 18 months, that is, at most 5 to 8 man years of available effort. With larger projects the increase in the communication effort required on the one side and the decreased visibility of the product on the other, means that the progress and control of the project are more difficult.

Project Phases

In order to increase the visibility and consistency of the software product, every project (itself as limited in extent as possible) should be laid down in a number of clear development phases. Each phase must be completed before work can start on the next. The result of each phase is a document containing all the information relating to this phase and which forms the starting point for the next phase. By this means the documentation becomes an integral part of the software development. The progress of the project can then be measured by the state and quality of the documentation. Figure 12.3 summarises the minimum number of development phases that should be identified in the execution

Project phase	Task	Result
System analysis and functional specification	Definition of − system function into primary and secondary requirements − statement of possible changes − external interfaces (input/output) − reliability parameters − test strategy (see ch.5)	Report on the functional specification
FUNCTIONAL BASE LINE		
Design specification	Definition of system design − file construction − functional description of individual software tools − functional descriptions of individual programs − inter-relationship of the programs − test plan − error handling	Report on the development specification − user's handbook − operator's handbook
DESIGN BASE LINE		
Programming	− Programming of the individual modules − Module testing − Program documentation	− Program listings − Program documentation
Testing integration and commissioning	− Integration of the individual modules − Structure and acceptance tests Documentation	− Complete system − Re-worked Documentation

Figure 12.3 Minimum number of project phases

of a software project. With more complex projects a finer resolution may be required (Mangold, 1974).

The divisions depicted in figure 12.3 are of particular importance to the supervision of the project and are discussed in the later sections of this chapter.

Figure 12.4 shows what percentage of the total effort has to be expended in each of the development phases. For on-line projects a rule of thumb for the subdivision is as follows

40 per cent for the functional specification and system design
20 per cent for coding and module testing
40 per cent for system test and final documentation.

The total effort required to bring a software project to its conclusion is strongly dependent on the complexity of the task as well as the quality and experience of the programmer team. This can be seen from the following example

Software Reliability

Activity	Informatics (%)	Raytheon (%)	TRW* (%)	Average (%)
Analysis	20	20	20	20
Design	16	20	20	18.7
Coding	16	25	24	21.7
Testing	32	25	28	28.3
Documentation	16	10	8	11.3
Overall Mathematical	(60)	(0)	(100)	(53.3)
Commercial	(40)	(100)	(0)	(46.7)

*Large variation from project to project

Figure 12.4 Subdivision of effort required for the various phases of a software project (Wolverton and Schick, 1972)

which shows the effort required to develop several FORTRAN compilers by the same project group (McClure, 1969).

Compiler No.	Estimated Effort (man months)	Actual Effort
1	36	72
2	24	36
3	12	14

In large software projects, that is, where more than about 25 programmers are working in parallel, there is a tendency for the individual differences in ability to average out, so that standard estimating procedures can be applied (Aron, 1970).

Project Teams

In answer to the question 'What constitutes the most important factor in a software project?' Boehm (1974a) states: 'Without doubt the quality of the personnel has the most important influence on a project.'

Because of the poor visibility of the product and the associated difficulty of supervision, a great part of the *de facto* responsibility must lie with the individual software specialists engaged in the actual performance of the task. It is thus necessary that this responsibility be supported by the relevant form of organisation.

A very successful attempt in this direction has been made with the 'chief programmer team' (Baker and Mills, 1973; IBM, 1971). With this type of organisation the entire technical responsibility is given to the highest qualified programmer who designs and codes the most important parts of the program. This chief programmer is supported by backup and junior programmers who work on the less important parts of the program. Administrative work is carried out by the programming secretary who also is responsible for documentation, test runs and project progress documentation.

This form of organisation allows the following objectives to be more easily achieved.

(1) *Reliability*   Higher reliability results from the uniformity of the structure which is overseen by the chief programmer.
(2) *Productivity*   As well as increased reliability, increased productivity may be seen to result from the use of a chief programmer team type of organisation. The programmer is able to develop his full potential, because he has technical responsibility while being largely relieved of administrative tasks.
(3) *Responsibility*   Responsibility for the project lies with those who have made the technical decisions, namely the programmers.

12.3 CONTROL

In this context project control is taken to mean the determination of progress against the project plan and the taking of corrective measures in the event of deviation, so that the planned objectives can still be attained in the light of the altered circumstances. The more pronounced the difference between the individual abilities of the programmers, and the less exact the basis of the planning, then the tighter is the control that is required. Under such conditions greater deviations must be expected which will require stronger corrective measures. However, tight control encroaches on the technical freedom of the individual, which can have a negative influence on creativity and motivation. Finding an equitable middle way is one of the greatest challenges of software management.

During a large part of the project development, progress can only be measured from the available documentation. It is therefore a prerequisite of project control that the documentation be developed in parallel to the actual software.

Documentation

While the first three documents (general description, user's handbook, and operator's manual) are necessary for any successful software product, the other documentation (functional specification, development specification, and program documentation) represents the essential prerequisites for the project control and software maintenance. Figure 12.5 shows which documents are required for each

Document	Content	Target readership	Format
General description	Description of most important system functions	Management and potential users	Easily understood prose
User's handbook	Description of all system functions	User	Text with many examples Index (user's notation)
Operator's handbook	Operating procedures Possible error messages and expected reaction	Operator	Flowcharts Examples (installation standards important)
Functional specification	Complete and detailed definition of all system functions	Users Programmers	Decision tables Text
Design specification	Internal construction of the software system and files Central flow	Programmers	Flowcharts Tables
Program specification	Program description Variable lists	Programmers	Commented listings, flow charts if necessary

Figure 12.5 Summary of the most important documentation that should be produced in a software project

project phase. If such a schedule is maintained, then in the majority of cases only a minimum of reworking of the documentation is required, after the system is delivered, in order to achieve its final state.

The quality of the documentation is a good indicator to the quality of the software. Good documentation should be precise, to the point, and complete. It should be aimed at a typical member of the intended readership, and avoid long-winded explanations. The documentation should have a structured hierarchy so that information can be found at the required level of detail, and changes can be introduced easily and quickly. Documentation that is not continuously updated and does not reflect the latest state is virtually worthless.

The design specification should contain not only information on the internal construction of the program but also a discussion of the reasons leading to this construction. It is much easier to introduce changes that conform to the structure if the original reasoning is available.

Good documentation can arise only from a well-structured system. If the software possesses a poor structure, then even a great effort on the documentation will not produce a clear end result. If the documentation of a software system tends to become too complex, then it is better to redo parts of the software (Kernighan and Plauger, 1974b).

Changes

Certain dynamics can be associated with almost every software project. Assumptions have to be made and later changed, suggested solutions that were implemented initially have to be modified and perhaps eventually abandoned. Software cannot be developed linearly but as a number of iterations. It is one of the most important tasks of project control to keep the iterations within reasonable bounds, keeping flexibility on the one hand and good co-ordination on the other. If the management has no understanding of these necessary iterations in the development process, then valuable knowledge gained during the development often cannot be used in a subsequent improvement of the system structure, and the first choice gets unjustified preference. On the other hand, too great a concentration on better ideas can lead to project delays. There are two main reasons for having to introduce changes

(1) new knowledge and requirements on the part of the user (see chapter 5), and
(2) the dynamics of the system design (see chapter 6).

It is the responsibility of project control to ensure that these change requests are limited to the current phase of the project and do not spread throughout the whole development process (see figure 12.6). To this end the base line software management technique has been developed (Piligian and Pokorney, 1967; Liebowitz, 1967; Ellingson, 1973). This management technique involves drawing dividing lines between the various development phases where the state of the development is bounded and frozen. Figure 12.3 shows two such base lines, the

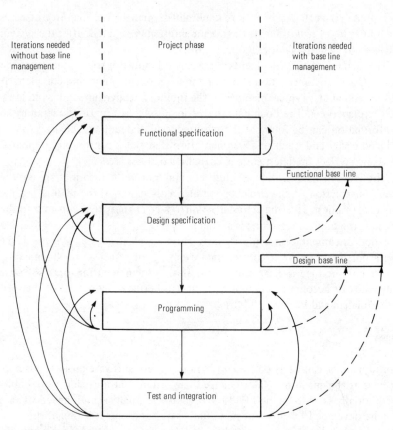

Iterations needed
without base line
management

Project phase

Iterations needed
with base line
management

Functional specification

Functional base line

Design specification

Design base line

Programming

Test and integration

Figure 12.6   Iterations that are required with and without base line management

functional line and the design line. With bigger projects further base lines are required, for example, an interface line. A particular design phase can only be said to have been completed when a particular base line has been reached. This can take place in a more or less formal way, when all the documentation relevant to a particular base line (see figure 12.3) has been checked and released by an independent monitor group. Simultaneously with reaching a base line, a procedure must be determined for the updating of the documentation that has to be frozen at the base line. The following is an example of how such a change procedure might be implemented.

(1)   The initiator of the change requests who considers them necessary submits them in written form, with suitable justification.

(2)   These are assessed by both the user and the system developer, and the consequences for overall function, costs and delivery dates are considered.

(3)   After the change requests have been submitted a high-level management

decision has to be made as to whether these changes will be carried out, as a result of which the consequences of the proposed changes are made known.

Through this form of organisation, which is concerned with overstepping base lines, the following should be achieved.

(1)　Before drawing a base line all available documentation has to be thoroughly checked by all parties concerned.
(2)　After a base line has been established only those changes are proposed that are absolutely essential.
(3)　Any subsequent changes are fully documented.
(4)　The consequences of a change are known beforehand.

The use of the base line technique means that the number of changes that spread through several development phases is greatly reduced, without substantially restricting the freedom of movement required during the more critical development phases. There are thus positive influences on the documentation, the software structure and finally the software reliability.

References and Selected Bibliography

Aron, J. D., 'Estimating Resources for Large Programming Systems', in *Software Engineering Techniques*, ed. J. N. Buxton and B. Randell (NATO Science Committee, Rome, 1970) pp. 68–79.

Avizienis, A., 'The Methodology of Fault Tolerant Computing', *Proceedings of the USA Japan Computer Conference* (1972) pp. 405–13.

Avizienis, A., 'Fault Tolerance and Fault Intolerance – Complementary Approaches to Reliable Computing', *Proceedings of the International Conference on Reliable Software*, (Los Angeles, 1975) pp. 458–64.

Avizienis, A., 'Fault Tolerance: The Survival Attribute of Digital Systems', *Proc. IEEE*, 66, No. 10 (1978) pp. 1109–25.

Baker, F. T., 'System Quality through Structured Programming', *Proceedings of the Fall Joint Computer Conference*, (AFIPS Press, 1972) pp. 339–42.

Baker, F. T., and Mills, H. D., 'Chief Programmer Teams', *Datamation*, 19 (1973) pp. 58–61.

Ball, M., and Hardie, F., 'Effects and Detection of Intermittent Faults in Digital Systems', *Proceedings of the Spring Joint Computer Conference*, (AFIPS Press, 1969) pp. 329–35.

Balzers, R. M., 'EXDAMS, Extendable Debugging and Monitoring System', *Proceedings of the Spring Joint Computer Conference* (AFIPS Press, 1969) pp. 567–80.

Belady, L. A., and Lehman, M. M., 'Programming Systems Dynamics or the Metadynamics of Systems in Maintenance and Growth', *IBM Research Report RC 3546* (1971).

Belady, L. A., and Lehman, M. M., 'An Introduction to Growth Dynamics', in *Statistical Computer Performance Evaluation*, ed. W. Freiberger (Academic Press, New York, 1972) pp. 503–11.

Boehm, B. W., *Proceedings of the TRW Symposium on Reliable, Cost-Effective, Secure Software*, *TRW Software Series Report TRW–SS–74–14*, (Redondo Beach, Calif., 1974a).

Boehm, B. W., 'Some Steps Toward Formal and Automated Aids to Software Requirements Analysis and Design', *Proceedings of the IFIP Conference* (Stockholm, 1974b) pp. 192–7.

Boehm, B. W., Brown, J. R., Kaspar, H., Lipow, M., MacLeod, G. J., and Merrit, M. J., 'Characteristics of Software Quality', *TRW Software Series Report TRW–SS–73–09*, (Redondo Beach, Calif., 1973).

Boehm, B. W., McClean, R. K., and Urfrig, D. B., 'Some Experience with Automated Aids to the Design of Large Scale Reliable Software', *Proceedings of the International Conference on Reliable Software* (Los Angeles, 1975) pp. 105–13.

Böhm, C., and Jacopini, G., 'Flow Diagrams, Turing Machines and Languages with only two Formation Rules', *Communs ACM*, 9, No. 5 (1966) pp. 366–71.

Boyd, R., 'Restoral of a Real Time Operating System', *Proceedings of the 1971 ACM National Conference* (Chicago, 1971) pp. 109–11.

Brinch Hansen, P., 'Structured Multiprogramming', *Communs ACM*, 15, No. 7 (1972) pp. 574–8.

Brinch Hansen, P., *Operating Systems Principles* (Prentice-Hall, Englewood Cliffs, N. J., 1973a).

Brinch Hansen, P., 'Testing a Multiprogramming System', *Software Practice and Experience*, 3 (1973b) pp. 145–50.

Brinch Hansen, P., *The Architecture of Concurrent Programs* (Prentice-Hall, Englewood Cliffs, N. J., 1977).

Brooks, F. P., 'The Mythical Man Months', *Datamation*, 20 (1974) pp. 45–52.

Carter, W. C., Jessop, D. C., Bouricius, W. G., Wadia, A. B., McCarthy, C. E., and Milligan, F. G., 'Design Techniques for Modular Architecture for Reliable Computer Systems', *IBM Report 70–208–0002*, (IBM Thomas J. Watson Research Center, 1970).

Carter, W. C., Wadia, A. B., Schneider, P. R., and Bouricius, W. G., 'Logic Design for Dynamic and Interactive Recovery', *IEEE Trans. Computers*, C–20, No. 11 (1971) pp. 1300–5.

Chandy, K. M., Browne, J. C., Dissly, C. W., and Uhrig, W. R., 'Analytic Models for Rollback and Recovery in Data Base Systems', *IEEE Trans. Software Engng*, SE–1, No. 1 (1975) pp. 100–10.

Coffman, E. G., and Denning, P. J., *Operating Systems Theory* (Prentice-Hall, Englewood Cliffs, N. J., 1973).

Coffman, E. G., Elphick, M. J., and Shoshani, A., 'System Deadlocks', *Comput. Surv.*, 3, No. 2 (1971) pp. 67–78.

Connet, J. R., Pasternak, E. J., and Wagner, B. D., 'Software Defenses in Real Time Systems', Digest of Papers of the 1972 IEEE International Symposium on Fault Tolerant Computing, (Newton, Mass., June 1972) pp. 94–9.

Corlieu, J. D., 'System Effectiveness', *Proceedings of the 1972 Annual Reliability and Maintainability Symposium* (1972) pp. 347–57.

Cougar, J. R., 'Evolution of Business Systems Analysis Techniques', *Comput. Sur.*, 5, No. 3 (1973), pp. 167–98.

Denning, P. J., 'Third Generation Computer Systems', *Comput. Sur.*, 3, No. 4 (1971) pp. 175–216.

Denning, P. J., 'Structuring Operating Systems for Reliability', *Infotech State of the Art Report No. 20* (Computer System Reliability, Infotech Ltd, Maidenhead, Berks, 1974a) pp. 481–504.

Denning, P. J., 'Is it not Time to Define Structured Programming?', *ACM Operating Systems Review*, 8, No. 1 (1974b), pp. 6–7.

Denning, P. J., 'Fault Tolerant Operating Systems', *Comput. Sur.*, 8, No. 4 (1976) pp. 359–90.

Dennis, J. B., 'Modularity', in *Advanced Course on Software Engineering*, ed. F. L. Bauer (Springer Verlag, Heidelberg 1973) pp. 128–82.

Dijkstra, E. W., 'GOTO Statements Considered Harmful', *Communs ACM*, 11, No. 3 (1968a), pp. 147–8.

Dijkstra, E. W., 'Cooperating Sequential Processes', in *Programming Languages* ed. F. Genuys (Academic Press, London, 1968b).

Dijkstra, E. W., 'Notes on Structured Programming', in *Structured Programming*, ed. E. W. Dijkstra, O. J. Dahl and C. A. R. Hoare, (Academic Press, London, 1972a) pp. 1–82.

Dijkstra, E. W., 'The Humble Programmer', *Communs ACM*, 15, No. 10 (1972b) pp. 859–66.

Dijkstra, E. W., *A Discipline of Programming* (Prentice-Hall, Englewood Cliffs, N. J., 1975).

Ellingson, O. E., 'Computer Program and Change Control', *Record of 1973 IEEE Symposium on Computer Software Reliability* (1973) pp. 82–9.

Elspas, B., Green, M. W., and Levitt, K. N., 'Software Reliability', *Computer*, 4, No. 1 (1971) pp. 21–7.

Endres, 'An Analysis of Errors and Their Causes in System Programs' *IEEE Trans. Software Engng*, SE–1, No. 2 (1975) pp. 40–9.

Floyd, R. W., 'Assigning Meanings to Programs', in *Mathematical Aspects of Computer Science*, ed. J. T. Schwartz, 19 (New York, 1967) pp. 19–32.

Fontao, R., 'Concurrent Algorithms for Avoiding Deadlocks in Multiprocessing Systems', *SIGOPS Operating Systems Review*, 6, No. 1, 2 (1972) p. 167.

Fragola, J. R., and Spahn, J. F., 'The Software Error Effect Analysis, a Qualitative Design Tool', *Record of 1973 IEEE Symposium on Computer Software Reliability* (1973) pp. 90–3.

Gelenbe, E., and Derochette, D., 'Performance of Rollback Recovery Systems under Intermittent Failures', *Communs ACM*, 21, No. 6 (1978) pp. 493–9.

Gerhard, S., and Yelowitz, L., 'Observations of Fallibility in Applications of Modern Programming Methodologies', *IEEE Trans. Software Engng*, SE–2, No. 3 (1976) pp. 195–207.

Geschke, C. M., and Mitchell, J. G., 'On the Problem of Uniform References to Data Structures', *Proceedings of the International Conference on Reliable Software* (Los Angeles, 1975) pp. 31–42.

Gibson, C. G., and Railing, L. R., 'Verification Guidelines', *TRW Software Series Report TRW–SS–71–04*, (Redondo Beach, Calif., 1971).

Gilb, T., *Reliable EDP Application Design* (Akademisk Forlag, Kobenhaven, 1973).

Goodenough, J. B., and Gerhart, S., 'Toward a Theory of Test Data Selection' *IEEE Trans. Software Engng*, SE–1, No. 2 (1975) pp. 156–73.

Goos, G., 'Hierarchies', in *Advanced Course on Software Engineering*, ed. F. L. Bauer (Springer Verlag, Heidelberg, 1973) pp. 29–46.

Grisham, R., 'The Debugging System Aids', *Proceedings of the Spring Joint Computer Conference 1970*, (AFIPS Press, 1971) pp. 59–64.

Hamilton, P. A., and Musa, J. D., 'Measuring Reliability of Computer Center Software', *Proceedings of the Third International Conference on Software Engineering*, (Atlanta, Georgia, 1978) pp. 29–38.

Hartman, W., Mathes, H., and Proeme, A., *Management Information Systems Handbook*, (McGraw-Hill, New York, 1968).

Havender, J. W., 'Avoiding Deadlocks in Multitasking Systems', *IBM System Journal*, 7, No. 2 (1968) pp. 74–84.

Head, R. V., 'Automated Systems Analysis' *Datamation*, 17 (1971) pp. 22–4.

Hecht, 'Fault Tolerant Software for Real Time Applications', *Comput. Surv.*, 8, No. 4 (1976) pp. 391–407.

Higgins, A. N., 'Error Recovery Through Programming', *Proceedings of the Fall Joint Computer Conference* (AFIPS Press, 1968) pp. 39–43.

Hill, I. D., 'Faults in Functions in ALGOL and FORTRAN', *Comput. J.*, 14, No. 3 (1971).

Hoare, C. A. R., 'Monitors: an Operating Systems Structuring Concept', *Communs ACM*, 17, No. 10 (1974) pp. 549–57.

Hoare, C. A. R., 'Data Reliability', *Proceedings of the International Conference on Reliable Software* (Los Angeles, 1975) pp. 528–33.

Holt, R. C., 'On Deadlock in Computer Sytems' (PhD Thesis, Cornell University, 1971).

Hopkins, M. E., in *Software Engineering Techniques*, ed. J. N. Buxton and B. Randell, (NATO Science Committee, Rome, 1970) p. 20.

Horning, J. J., and Randell, B., 'Process Structuring', *Comput. Surv.*, 5, No. 1 (1973) pp. 5–30.

Horning, J. J., Lauer, H. C., Melliar Smith, P. M., and Randell, B., 'A Program Structure for Error Detection and Recovery', *Proceedings of the Conference on Operating Systems: Theoretical and Practical Aspects* (IRIA, Rocenquourt, 1974) pp. 177–93.

Hoskyns Systems Research Inc., 'Implications of Using Modular Programming', *Guide No. 1* (New York, 1973).

Howden, W. E., 'Theoretical and Empirical Studies of Program Testing', *Proceedings of the Third International Conference on Software Engineering*, (Atlanta, Georgia, 1978) pp. 306–11.

IBM, Study Organization Plan (SOP), Form No. C 20–8075 (White Plains, N. Y., 1961).

IBM, Chief Programmer Teams, 'Principles and Procedures', *Report FSC–71–5108*, (IBM Federal Systems Division, Gaithersburg, Md; 1971).

Jackson, M., 'Mnemonics', *Datamation*, 13 (1967) pp. 26–8.

Jackson, M. A., *Principles of Program Design*, (Academic Press, 1975).

Jelinski, Z., and Moranda, P., 'Software Reliability Research', in *Statistical Computer Performance Evaluation*, ed. W. Freiberger (Academic Press, New York, 1972) pp. 465–84.

Katsuki, D., Elsam, E. S., Mann, W. F., Roberts, E. S., Robonson, J. G., Skowronski, F. S., and Wolf, E. W., 'Pluribus An Operational Fault Tolerant Multiprocessor', *Proc. IEEE*, 66, No. 10 (1978) pp. 1146–59.

Kernighan, B. W., and Plauger, P. J., *The Elements of Programming Style*, (McGraw-Hill, New York, 1974a).

Kernighan, B. W., and Plauger, P. J., 'Programming Style: Examples and Counter Examples', *Comput. Surv.* 6, No. 4 (1974b) pp. 302–19.

King, J. C., 'Proving Programs to be Correct', *IEEE Trans. Computers*, C–20, No. 11 (1971) pp. 1131–6.

Knuth, D. E., 'An Empirical Study of FORTRAN Programs', *Software Practice and Experience*, 1, No. 2 (1971) pp. 105–33.

Knuth, D. E., 'Structured Programming with GOTO Statements', *Comput. Surv.*, 6, No. 4 (1974) pp. 261–302.

Kopetz, H., 'Software Redundancy in Real Time Systems', *Proceedings of the IFIP Congress*, (Stockholm, 1974) pp. 182–6.

Kopetz, H., 'On the Connections Between Range of Variable and Control Structure Testing', *Proceedings of the International Conference on Reliable Software* (Los Angeles, 1975a) pp. 511–17.

Kopetz, H., 'Systematic Error Treatment in Real Time Software', *Proceedings of the IFAC Congress* (Boston, 1975b) pp. 39.1/1–8.

Kopetz, H., 'System Reliability and Software Redundancy', *Infotech State of the Art Report on Real Time Software* (Infotech Ltd, Maidenhead, 1976).

Liebowitz, B. H., 'The Technical Specification – Key to Management Control of Computer Programming', *Proceedings of the Spring Joint Computer Conference* (AFIPS Press, 1967) pp. 51–9.

Linden, T. A., Operating System Structures to Support Security and Reliable Software, *Comput. Surv.*, 8, No. 4, (1976) pp. 409–45.

Lindhorst, W. M., 'Scheduled Maintenance of Application Software', *Datamation*, 19 (1973) pp. 64–7.

Liskov, B. H., and Zilles, S. N., 'Specification Techniques for Data Abstraction', *IEEE Trans. Software Engng*, SE–1, No. 1 (1975) pp. 7–18.

Littlewood, B., 'How to Measure Software Reliability and How Not To', *Proceedings of the Third International Conference on Software Engineering* (Atlanta, Georgia, 1978) pp. 39–45.

Lomet, D. B., 'Process Structuring, Synchronisation and Recovery Using Atomic Actions', in *Proceedings ACM Conference on Language Design for Reliable Software*, SIGPLAN Notices 12, No. 3 (1977) pp. 128–37.

London, R. L., 'A View of Program Verification', *Proceedings of the International Conference on Reliable Software* (Los Angeles, 1975) pp. 534–45.

MacWilliams, W. H., 'Reliability of Large Real Time Control Software Systems', *Record of the 1973 IEEE Symposium on Computer Software Reliability* (1973) pp. 1–6.

Mangold, E. R., 'Software Visibility and Management', *Proceedings of the TRW Symposium on Cost Effective, Reliable, Secure Software* (Redondo Beach, Calif., 1974) pp. 2.1–2.25.

Manna, Z., 'The Correctness of Computer Programs', *J. Comput. Syst. Sci. 3* (1969) pp. 119–27.

Martin, J., *System Analysis for Data Transmission* (Prentice-Hall, Englewood Cliffs, N. J., 1972).

Martin, J. J., 'Generalized Structured Programming', *Proceedings of the National Computer Conference* (AFIPS Press, 1974) pp. 665–9.

McClure, R. M., 'Projections versus Performance in Software Production', in *Software Engineering*, ed. P. Naur and B. Randell (NATO Science Committee, Rome, 1969).

Metzelaar, P. N., 'Cost Estimation Graph', (TRW Systems Group, Redondo Beach, Calif., 1971).

Mills, H. D., 'Mathematical Foundations of Structured Programming', *IBM Report FSC 72–6012* (Federal Systems Division, IBM Gaithersburg, Md, 1972).

Mills, H. D., 'The Complexity of Programs', in *Program Test Methods*, ed. W. C. Hetzel (Prentice-Hall, Englewood Cliffs, N. J., 1973) pp. 225–38.

Mills, H. D., 'How to Write Correct Programs and Know It', *Proceedings of the International Conference on Reliable Software* (Los Angeles, 1975) pp. 363–70.

Myers, G. J., 'Characteristics of Composite Design', *Datamation*, 19, No. 9 (1973) pp. 100–2.

Myers, G. J., *Software Reliability, Principles and Practice*, (Wiley, New York, 1976).

Neumann, P., Goldberg, J., Levitt, K. N., and Wensley, J. H., 'A Study of Fault Tolerant Computing', *Final Report SRI Project 1693*, (Stanford Research Instititue, 1973).

Ogdin, J. L., 'Designing Reliable Software', *Datamation*, 18 (1972) pp. 71–8.

Parnas, D. L., 'Information Distribution Aspects of Design Methodology', *Proceedings of the IFIP Congress* (Ljubljana, 1971) pp. 339–44.

Parnas, D. L., 'On the Criteria to be Used in Decomposing Systems into Modules', *Communs ACM*, 15, No. 12 (1972a) pp. 1053–8.

Parnas, D. L., 'A Technique of Software Module Specification with Examples', *Communs ACM*, 15, No. 5 (1972b) pp. 330–6.

Peters, L. J., 'Software Design, Current Methods and Techniques', *Proceedings of the Infotech State of the Art Conference "Beyond Structural Programming"* (Atlanta, 1978) pp. 4-1-4-24.

Piligian, H. S., and Pokorney, J. L., 'Air Force Concepts for the Technical Control and Design Verification of Computer Programs', *Proceedings of the Spring Joint Computer Conference*, (AFIPS Press, 1967) pp. 61–6.

Ramamoorthy, C. V., and Ho, S. F., 'Testing Large Software with Automated Software Evaluation Systems', *IEEE Trans. Software Engng*, SE–1, No. 1 (1975) pp. 46–58.

Randell, B., 'Operating Systems, the Problems of Performance and Reliability', *Proceedings of the IFIP Congress* (Ljubljana, 1971) pp. I.100–I.109.

Randell, B., 'System Structure for Software Fault Tolerance', *IEEE Trans.*

Software Engng, SE–1, No. 2 (1975) pp. 220–32.

Randell, B., Lee, P. A., and Treleaven, M. P. C., 'Reliability Issues in Computing System Design', *Comput. Surv.*, 10, No. 2 (1978) pp. 123–66.

Rault, J. C., 'Extension of Hardware Fault Detection Models to the Verification of Software', in *Program Test Methods*, ed. W. C. Hetzel, (Prentice-Hall, Englewood Cliffs, N. J., 1973) pp. 255–62.

Roos, D. T., and Shoman, K. E., 'Structured Analysis for Requirements Definition', *IEEE Trans. Software Engng*, SE–3, No. 1 (1977) pp. 6–15.

Rubey, R. J., 'Quantitative Aspects of Software Validation', *Proceedings of the International Conference on Reliable Software* (Los Angeles, 1975) pp. 246–51.

Sackman, H., *Man Computer Problem Solving* (Auerbach, 1970).

Sadowski, W. L., and Lozier, D. W., 'A Unified Standards Approach to Algorithm Testing', in *Program Test Methods*, ed. W. C. Hetzel (Prentice-Hall, Englewood Cliffs, N. J., 1973) pp. 277–90.

Scherr, A. L., 'Testing Large Software Systems', in *Program Test Methods*, ed. W. C. Hetzel (Prentice-Hall, Englewood Cliffs, N. J., 1973) pp. 165–80.

Schwartz, J. I., 'Analyzing Large Scale System Development', in *Software Engineering Techniques*, ed. J. N. Buxton and B. Randell, (NATO Science Committee, Rome, 1970) pp. 122–37.

Schwartz, J. T., 'An Overview of Bugs', in *Debugging Techniques in Large Systems*, ed. R. Rusting (Prentice-Hall, Englewood Cliffs, N. J., 1971) pp. 1–16.

Shooman, M. L., 'Structural Models for Software Reliability Prediction', *Proceedings of the Second International Conference on Software Engineering* (San Francisco, 1976) pp. 268–75.

Shooman, M. L., and Bolsky, M. I., 'Types, Distribution, and Test and Correction Times for Programming Errors', *Proceedings of the International Conference on Software Reliability* (Los Angeles, 1975) pp. 347–57.

Seegmuller, G., 'Systems Programming as Emerging Discipline', *Proceedings of the IFIP Congress* (Stockholm, 1974) pp. 419–27.

Simon, H. A., 'The Architecture of Complexity', *Proc. Am. phil. Soc.*, 106 (1962) pp. 467–82.

Simon, H. A., 'The Theory of Problem Solving', *Proceedings of the IFIP Congress* (Ljubljana, 1971) pp. I.249–I.266.

Sloughter, J. B., 'Understanding the Software Problem', *Proceedings of the National Computer Conference* (AFIPS Press, 1974) pp. 331–6.

Smith, J. L., and Holden, T. S., 'Restart of an Operating System having a Permanent File Structure', *Comput. J.*, 15, No. 1 (1972) pp. 25–31.

Spier, M. J., 'A Prognostic Proposal for the Improvement of Program Modularity and Reliability' (Private Communications, 1975).

Spooner, C. R., 'A Software Architecture for the 70, Part I., The General Approach', *Software Practice and Experience*, 1, No. 1 (1971) pp. 5–37.

Stevens, W. P., Myers, G. J., and Constantine, L. L., 'Structured Design', *IBM Syst. J.*, 13 (1974) pp. 115–39.

Teichroew, D., and Hershey, E. A., 'PSL/PSA A Computer Aided Technique for Structured Documentation and Analysis of Information Processing Systems', *IEEE Trans. Software Engng*, SE–3, No. 1 (1977) pp. 41–9.

Toy, W. N., 'Fault Tolerant Design of Local ESS Processors', *Proc. IEEE*, 66, No. 10 (1978) pp. 1126–45.

Turski, W. M., in *Notes from a Workshop on the Attainment of Reliable Software*, ed. D. B. Wortman, *Technical Report CSRG 41* (Computer Systems Research Group, University of Toronto, 1974).

Verhofstad, J. S. M., 'Recovery Techniques for Database Systems', *Comput. Surv.*, 10, No. 2 (1978) pp. 167–96.

Walker, L. L., 'Systems Availability', in *Infotech State of the Art Report No. 20, Computer Systems Reliability*, (Infotech Ltd, Maidenhead, 1974) pp. 253–71.

Weinberg, G. M., *The Psychology of Computer Programming*, (Van Nostrand Reinhold, New York, 1971).

Weissmann, L. M., 'A Methodology for Studying the Complexity of Computer Programs', *Report No. CSRG 37* (Computer Systems Research Group, University of Toronto, 1974).

Wensley, J. J., Lamport, L., Goldberg, J., Green, M. W., Levitt, K. N., Melliar Smith, P. M., Shostak, R. E. and Weinstok, C. B., 'SIFT: The Design and Analysis of a Fault-Tolerant Computer for Aircraft Control', *Proc. IEEE*, 66, No. 10 (1978) pp. 1240–54.

Williman, A. O., and Donnel, C. O., 'Through the Central Multiprocessor Avionics Enters the Computer Era), *Astronaut. Aeronaut.*, 8 (1970) pp. 216–20.

Wirth, N., 'On Multiprogramming, Machine Coding and Computer Organization', *Communs ACM*, 12, No. 9 (1969) pp. 488–98.

Wolverton, R. W., 'The Cost of Developing Large Scale Software', *IEEE Trans. Comput*, C-23, No. 6 (1974), pp. 615–36.

Wolverton, R. W., and Schick, G. J., 'Assessment of Software Reliability', *TRW Software Report, Software Series TRW SS 72 04*, (Redondo Beach, Calif., 1972).

Woodger, M., 'On Semantic Levels in Programming', *Proceedings of the IFIP Congress*, (Ljubljana, 1971) pp. TA–3–79–84.

Wulf, W., Cohen, E., Corwin, W., Jones, A., Levin, R., Pierson, C., and Pollack, F., 'HYDRA: The Kernel of a Multiprocessor Operating System', *Communs ACM*, 17, No. 6 (1974) pp. 337–44.

Zilles, S. N., in 'Notes from a Workshop on the Attainment of Reliable Software', ed. D. B. Wortman, *Technical Report CSRG–41*, (Computer Systems Research Group, University of Toronto, 1974).

Zurcher, F. W., and Randell, B., 'Multilevel Modelling – A Methodology for Computer Design', *Proceedings of the IFIP Congress* (Edinburgh, 1968) pp. 867–71.

Index